2/18

DATE DUE

The Library Store #47-0119

TAQUERÍA

TACOS

A TACO COOKBOOK
TO BRING THE FLAVORS OF MEXICO HOME

Leslie Limón

ROCKRIDGE
PRESS

Front cover photography © StockFood / Linsell, Samantha

Back cover photography © Stocksy/Gabriel (Gabi) Bucataru

Interior photography © Stockfood/Samantha Linsell, Cover; Stockfood/Samantha Linsell, p.2; Stockfood/Tanya Zouev, p.7; Stocksy/Pixel Stories, p.8; Stocksy/Sean Locke, p.19; Stocksy/Martí Sans, p.21; Stocksy/Darren Muir, p.22; Stocksy/Gabriel (Gabi) Bucataru, p.34; Stockfood/Rua Castilho, p.60; Shutterstock/Joshua Resnick, p.91; Stockfood/Eisin Studio - Food Photo & Video, p.92; Stockfood/James Franco, p.108; Stockfood/Pepe Nilsson, p.128; Stockfood/Jim Norton, p.148; Shutterstock/Foodio, p.181; Stockfood/Fotos mit Geschmack, p.182; Stocksy/Sara Remington, p.202.

ISBN: Print 978-1-62315-751-7 | eBook 978-1-62315-752-4

CONTENTS

INTRODUCTION

So much more than the version popularized by fast-food restaurants (a shell filled with refried beans and ground beef, topped with lettuce and bright orange cheese), tacos are the ultimate Mexican comfort food. Even in their simplest form, they are mouth-wateringly irresistible.

Raised by my Mexican grandparents in Redlands, California, I grew up eating home-made, authentic Mexican food from Sonora and Chihuahua states. My earliest taco memories are of helping roll balls of *masa* (dough) and flattening them in a tortilla press while my grandmother gently laid them on a hot cast iron *comal* (griddle). Imagine handmade corn tortillas hot off the comal, filled with juicy pieces of spice-rubbed steak grilled to perfection, perfectly garnished with chopped onion and cilantro, and topped with a squeeze of fresh lime juice and fiery roasted tomatillo

salsa. Tacos are happiness wrapped in warm tortillas, and this book is a celebration of all things tacos—because a life without tacos is no life at all.

Tacos are a fun and easy meal to serve for breakfast, lunch, and dinner. Almost everything you have in your pantry and refrigerator can be used in tacos. *Tacos Dorados de Papa* (page 174) is my go-to meal when I need to get dinner ready in a hurry. And black bean tacos with crumbled *queso fresco* and *pico de gallo* are a budget-friendly dinner option the whole family will love. What I love the most about tacos is that they can be enjoyed whether you're home alone and just want something quick and simple to eat, or when you're hosting a *fiesta* (celebration) for family and friends.

This cookbook is for anyone who wants to eat tacos more often, as well as anyone who wants to learn to make a wide range of delicious, authentic Mexican tacos. From tortillas, tasty fillings and salsas, and classic side dishes to traditional *aguas frescas* (fresh waters) and heady margaritas, you'll be able to recreate the flavor and aromas of traditional *taquerías* (taco stands) in your *cocina* (kitchen).

To start off, we'll cover taco basics: the tools you'll need in the kitchen, the different types of tacos, a guide to Mexican *quesos* (cheeses), and menu suggestions for hosting your own *taquiza* (taco bar). Chapter 2 offers step-by-step instructions on making tortillas from scratch. The chapters that follow showcase a variety of fillings, which can also be served on their own. Because we don't always have hours to spend in the kitchen, many of the recipes featured throughout the book can be prepared in 30 minutes or less;

just look for the Quick & Easy label. With so many tasty filling options, you'll be able to enjoy tacos every night of the week because, contrary to the popular hashtag, tacos aren't just for Tuesdays.

ONE
TACOS, A HOW-TO

▽▽▽▽▽ ▽▽▽▽ ▽ ▽▽▽▽▽▽ ▽ ▽ ▽▽▽▽▽▽ ▽ ▽ ▽▽▽▽ ▽

Quick and easy to prepare, a cutlery-free eating experience, and appropriate anytime of day, tacos are Mexico's most loved fast food, making it understandable why there's a taquería on almost every corner in Mexico. All you really need is a warm tortilla, any kind of filling—be it leftovers from last night's dinner, refried beans, or those carnitas (braised shredded pork) you scored at the Mexican market—and your favorite salsa or hot sauce. Score!

Growing up in a Mexican household, tacos weren't just a fast-food option. Tacos filled with refried beans, scrambled eggs, and pico de gallo were part of a hearty breakfast. Tacos de frijoles con queso (bean and cheese tacos) were what my grandmother lovingly packed for my lunch every day for school. And tacos became a late-night snack when I got home too late and missed out on Pappy's (my grandfather's) slow-cooked Barbacoa de Res (Mexican beef roast; page 39).

Before we get into the actual recipes, we need to go over a few basics. What tools do you really need to make tortillas? What seasonings should you always have on hand in your pantry? And what is the difference between queso fresco and queso asadero? You'll learn about all that and more. Like what tacos to make when you have only a few minutes to get dinner together. Or maybe you want to host a Mexican-themed fiesta and aren't sure what to serve. Not to worry! We've got menu suggestions for all your dinner and entertaining needs.

TOOLS OF THE TACOS

I've always believed tacos can be made with anything you have in your kitchen, and I don't just mean ingredient-wise. If you have a large frying pan or skillet, you can make tacos at home. But to bring a little of the taquería experience home, here are a few trusted tools of the taco trade.

COMAL

One of the oldest, most versatile tools used in Mexican kitchens for generations, and still widely used today, is the comal. A comal is a flat griddle used to cook or reheat tortillas, sear meat for tacos, and toast spices, chiles, tomatoes, and tomatillos for salsas. You can find the perfect comal to fit your needs, as they come in various shapes (round, square, or oval), sizes (ranging from 6 to 16 inches), and materials (clay, cast iron, and nonstick). During a trip to Mexico, my grandmother had a square cast iron comal custom-made to fit over the four burners of her stove so she could make her famous Sonoran-style flour tortillas.

PLANCHA

When it comes to making tacos, a *plancha* is a must. A large rectangular griddle made from either stainless steel or aluminum, a plancha is similar to a comal and is ideal for making a large number of tacos or when cooking for a crowd or fiesta. Most taquerías use a plancha for all their taco needs, from cooking tortillas *hechas a mano* (handmade) to sautéing onions and fresh chiles to frying *bistec* (thin-cut slices of steak), chorizo, chicken breast, or other meats.

MOLCAJETE

Made of volcanic rock or clay, this pre-Hispanic mortar and pestle is used to grind spices, chiles, and ingredients like garlic, tomatillos, and avocados to make salsas, sauces, and guacamoles. The bowl, or mortar, is the actual *molcajete*, while the pestle is called a *tejolote*. A molcajete can be used to make your salsa or guacamole, and it also makes a beautiful serving bowl. If you don't have molcajete, a blender or food processor will work just fine for grinding and mixing ingredients.

TORTILLADORA

A *tortilladora* (tortilla press) is used when making corn tortillas from scratch. It's the quickest, most efficient way to flatten balls of masa into thin, perfectly shaped circles. There are four types of tortillas presses you can find online: wooden, cast iron, aluminum, and sturdy plastic. Choosing the right tortilladora is a matter of personal preference. I've used all four kinds and they all get the job done. If you don't have a tortilladora, placing a ball of masa between two pieces of wax paper then flattening with a large, flat plate works just as well.

RODILLO

If you don't already have a *rodillo* (rolling pin) in your kitchen, this good old-fashioned tool is the best for rolling out flour tortillas.

LIME JUICER

Whether you're whipping up a tasty marinade, a refreshing margarita, or squeezing fresh lime juice over tacos or pico de gallo, this easy-to-use, handheld gadget is also one of the most used tools in my cocina.

METATE

Though used less today than in the pre-Hispanic era, this larger rectangular version of the molcajete is also made of volcanic rock and a great addition to the serious cook's collection. *Metates* are invaluable tools for those looking to add authentic Mexican flavor to their sauces. Metates are still used today to grind dried chiles for *moles, adobos* (marinades), and other salsas, as well as for grinding nixtamalized corn (dried corn that's been soaked and cooked in lime water) to make masa for tortillas, tamales, or *atoles* (warm Mexican porridge).

CHIQUIHUITE OR CANASTA

When lined with a clean, hand-embroidered kitchen towel, this small basket is used to hold freshly made tortillas and keep them warm. *Chiquihuites* lined with dried corn husks are also used as a mold to shape Mexican cheeses like queso fresco and *queso panela*. You can use a plastic *tortillero* (tortilla holder) or even a bowl to keep your tortillas warm, but using a small decorative *canasta* (basket) adds a touch of warmth and comfort to the table.

TIPOS DE TACOS

All tacos are not created equal. *Thank goodness!* Not only do tacos vary by filling, but also by the method in which they are cooked. Most tacos fall into one of the following categories:

Tacos al pastor: One of the most popular tacos in all of Mexico, *tacos al pastor* have endless layers of thinly sliced pork in a spicy marinade, topped with a whole pineapple, slow roasted in a gas or wood-burning *trompo* (spit). The juices of the pineapple help tenderize the meat while adding a touch of sweetness to the adobo.

Tacos al carbon: Also known as *tacos a la leña* and *tacos asados* and very popular in the northern region of Mexico, these are tacos with a grilled meat filling. Corn or flour tortillas are cooked on a comal placed atop the grill, with several accompaniments such as green onions, *nopales* (whole cactus paddles), and cheese-stuffed yellow peppers grilled alongside.

Tacos de pescado/mariscos: Popular in the coastal states, these fish and seafood tacos are prepared a number of ways, which you will learn about in chapter 4.

Tacos de guisados: A *guisado* is a traditional one-pot Mexican dish typically prepared in a *cazuela de barro* (clay pot) that can be served on its own as a main dish or as a filling for tacos, gorditas, and burritos. Some popular guisados are *Rajas con Crema* (roasted poblano strips in cream; page 125), *Chile Colorado* (page 46), *Camarones a la Mexicana* (Mexican-style shrimp; page 70), and *mole de pollo* (chicken mole). Tacos de guisados are popular throughout Mexico, although the types of guisados will vary from state to state. Tacos de guisados are ideal for a taquiza where the fillings are displayed buffet style and guests build their own tacos with their favorite guisados. In chapters 3 and 4, I share some of my most beloved guisados.

Tacos de canasta: Also known as *tacos sudados*, these tacos are filled with simple guisados like *Papas con Chorizo* (potatoes with chorizo; page 121), refried beans, shredded pork, *chicharrónes* (pork rinds) in red or green salsas, and *requesón* (similar to ricotta cheese), then lightly fried in *manteca* (lard) just until heated through. The tacos are stacked in a large canasta lined with layers of kitchen towels, plastic, and unwaxed paper to cover the tacos, trapping the heat inside to keep them warm.

Tacos dorados: Crunchy tacos do exist in Mexico, but they are nothing like the kind you find north of the border. *Tacos dorados* are crispy fried tacos made one of two ways. In the first technique, fill the tortilla with the filling of your choice, fold the tortilla in half to form the taco, and then fry the taco in oil. Serve topped with shredded cabbage, sliced or pickled red onion, and a tomato-based salsa. In the second technique, fry an unfilled folded tortilla in oil until crispy and golden. Once fried to a golden crisp, carefully open and fill the tortilla shell with shredded meats or guisados. Serve topped with crumbled queso fresco, shredded cabbage, a drizzling of Mexican crema, and spicy hot sauce. *Flautas* and *taquitos* also fall into the category of tacos dorados, which you'll learn more about in chapter 2.

Tacos placeros: *Tacos placeros* are the easiest kind of taco to prepare because the fillings require little to no cooking whatsoever, and even the garnishes are kept simple and light. For me, there is nothing more comforting than a warm corn tortilla with a slice of queso panela, a grilled *nopal* (cactus paddle), or maybe a few pieces of crispy chicharrónes topped with a spoonful of *Chile de Molcajete* (roasted tomatillo and chile de árbol salsa; page 132).

Tacos Árabes: Similar in preparation and flavor to tacos al pastor, *tacos Árabes* are served on pita bread instead of corn tortillas. Legend has it that tacos al pastor and tacos Árabes were inspired by the lamb shawarma prepared by Lebanese immigrants.

PREP & STORAGE

The following are a few helpful tips on how to handle, prepare, and store ingredients and recipes included throughout this book.

FRESH CHILES

Rinse chiles with cold water and pat them dry with paper towels. Store them in the refrigerator in an airtight container or sealed zip-top bag.

Always wear plastic gloves when handling fresh chiles, as the oil in the seeds and stem can cause an unpleasant burning sensation on the skin of your bare hands. If for some reason you've handled the chiles with your bare hands, avoid touching your face or eyes, and immediately rinse your hands with a mixture of soap, baking soda, and water.

DRIED CHILES

Store dried chiles in an airtight container in the pantry.

To remove stems and seeds from dried ancho, guajillo, pasilla, and chipotle chiles, cut off the tops of the dried chiles as close to the stem as possible, then remove the stem and shake out the dried seeds inside.

FRESH CILANTRO

To store fresh herbs like cilantro, rinse well with cold water and pat dry with paper towels. Wrap cilantro lightly with a dry paper towel and store in an unsealed zip-top bag in the refrigerator.

TORTILLAS

When making tortillas, I like to double the recipe so I have enough tortillas to last me through the week. Once the tortillas have cooled, stack and store them inside an airtight zip-top bag. Keep them in the refrigerator for up to seven days.

To freeze homemade tortillas, layer a piece of parchment paper between each of the tortillas to prevent them from sticking together. Store in freezer bags. Thaw frozen tortillas in the refrigerator at least one day before you'll need them.

MARINATED MEATS

Marinated meats like *Pork Chorizo* (page 56) and *Carne Adobada* (page 42) can be frozen once the marinade has been added. Divide uncooked marinated meat into two to four portions and wrap each tightly in freezer paper or freezer bags.

FILLINGS & GUISADOS

Let leftover fillings and guisados like *Tinga de Pollo* (page 90), *Cochinita Pibil* (page 52), *Ground Beef Picadillo* (page 53), and *Barbacoa de Res* (page 39), cool completely before storing them in airtight containers. Keep in the refrigerator for three to five days, or store in the freezer for four to six weeks. Let them thaw completely in the refrigerator.

COOKED BEANS

Cool *Frijoles de la Olla* (slow cooker beans; page 95) completely. Store in an airtight container in the refrigerator for up to one week. Or divide the beans into 2- to 4-cup portions and freeze in airtight containers. Thaw beans completely in the refrigerator.

SALADS

Store salads like *Ensalada de Nopales* (page 102) and *Black Bean Salad with Corn and Nopales* (page 103) in an airtight container and keep in the refrigerator for three to five days.

GARNISHES

Because everyone garnishes their tacos differently, there are bound to be leftovers. Store fresh garnishes like sliced onion, chopped cilantro, lime wedges, *Cebollas Encurtidas* (pickled red onions; page 131), *Pico de Gallo* (page 139), and shredded cabbage in separate airtight containers or plastic zip-top baggies. Keep in the refrigerator for three to five days. The same applies to grilled/cooked garnishes like *Cebollitas Asadas* (page 114), cooked nopales, and *Chiles Torreados* (page 135).

Store pickled garnishes like *Jalapeños en Escabeche* (page 138) in an airtight container and keep in the refrigerator for six to eight weeks.

SALSAS

Let salsas like *Chile de Molcajete* (page 132) and *Salsa Taquera Roja* (page 143) cool completely before storing in airtight containers. Refrigerate for up to one week, or store in the freezer for up to three months. Thaw in the refrigerator overnight.

AGUAS FRESCAS

Leftover agua frescas can be stored in an airtight pitcher or container for up to three days.

Or use leftover agua fresca to make *paletas* (ice pops) by pouring into paleta molds or Dixie cups. Cover the molds with aluminum foil and insert wooden ice pop sticks in the center of each mold. The aluminum foil prevents the ice pop sticks from moving around.

TACO SEASONINGS

Spices play an important role in the cocina, whether preparing an elaborate mole sauce, which can have up to 40 different ingredients, adding a bit of flavor to *Tortillas Rojas* (handmade chile-infused corn tortillas; page 31), or spicing hearty guisados like *Chile Colorado* (page 46). Dried chiles are also a must in the Mexican pantry, as they lend intense color; rich, earthy flavor; and varying levels of heat to traditional Mexican soups, guisados, and salsas. With these spices and dried chiles in your cocina, you can enjoy tacos every night of the week.

Mexican oregano: With light citrus undertones, dried Mexican oregano offers a more intense flavor and aroma than its Mediterranean counterpart. Mexican oregano adds a robust flavor to soups, stews, and marinades.

Cumin: This fragrant spice adds a distinct warm flavor to dry rubs, guisados, and rich salsas.

Cloves: While traditionally used in baked goods, cloves are one of the key spices in most mole sauces. It is also used in dry rubs for grilled meats.

Cinnamon: Cinnamon is one of the most versatile spices in the Mexican cocina, as it can be used in both sweet and savory dishes.

Black pepper: Whole black peppercorns are used to flavor soups, stews, and moles, while ground black pepper is used in dry rubs and marinades for meats, chicken, and fish. If you don't have whole black peppercorns on hand, don't worry—ground pepper will work.

Tajín: Not to be confused with chili powder, this spicy blend of ground chiles and salt flavored with lime is a delicious seasoning for fresh fruits, vegetables, and margaritas.

Sesame seeds: Toasted sesame seeds add a nutty flavor to mole sauces and other dried chile–based salsas. They also add a hint of crunchiness when used to garnish tacos.

Chile de árbol: This small dried chile, produced in the small town where I live, just north of Guadalajara, has a unique flavor, aroma, and spiciness unlike any other chile. Chile de árbol adds quite a bit of heat to salsas and marinades. If you are unable to find chile de árbol, cayenne pepper can be used as a substitute.

Ancho chiles: These dried poblano chiles are full of earthy flavor with a hint of sweetness. Ancho chiles offer the perfect balance between mild and spicy. They are used to add flavor and spice to soups, stews, sauces, and hearty meat dishes.

Guajillo chiles: Long, slim, and smooth, these chiles add an intense color to broths, although they tend to be very mild. New Mexico chiles are a great substitute.

Pasilla chiles: Long, dark chilaca chiles in dried form, pasillas have a sweet undertone similar to raisins with moderately spicy flavor. Pasillas are typically used to make *mole negro* and other sauces.

Dried chipotles: With an unmistakable smoky flavor, chipotles are dried smoked jalapeños. Add them to salsas and guisados.

Chipotles in adobo: Dried chipotle peppers packed in a vibrant red sauce are a quick and delicious way to add smoky heat to any dish.

Achiote paste: Sold in small squares or rectangles in the Latin food aisle of many supermarkets, achiote paste is made from ground annatto seeds, vinegar, garlic, and spices. It is the key ingredient in *Cochinita Pibil* (pork pibil, a traditional dish from the Yucatán Peninsula; page 52), but can also be used in dry rubs and marinades.

Mole paste: Because we don't always have time to make mole sauce from scratch, mole paste is one of my must-have pantry ingredients. Mole paste is a blend of dried chiles, Mexican chocolate, and spices.

Mexican chocolate: Sold in small discs called *tabletas*, Mexican chocolate is a combination of ground cocoa, granulated sugar, and cinnamon used to make sweet beverages and in savory dishes like moles and salsas.

Masa harina: A grainy textured corn flour used to make dough for tortillas and tamales, *masa harina* is also used to coat pan-fried meats and fish and as a thickening agent for stews and salsas.

QUESO PROFUNDO

Mexican cheeses are now much more readily available in the United States, but that wasn't always the case when I was growing up. My grandparents always brought an ice cooler full of fresh Mexican quesos on the drive home from visiting family in the border towns of Sonora. Most of the cheese was stored in the freezer, with the rest used to make quesadillas, enchiladas, flautas, and Pappy's famous *chile de rajas con queso* (a roasted chile pepper garnish with cheese).

Mexican cheeses range from soft, mild, and creamy to hard, pungent, and aged. Fresh Mexican cheeses like queso fresco, queso panela, and requesón are delicious served fresh with crackers or toasted *bolillo* (Mexican bread roll) slices for a Mexican cheese plate alongside a more flavorful cheese like *queso manchego*. If it's ooey, gooey melted goodness you're looking for, *queso Oaxaca*, queso asadero, and *queso Chihuahua* are the way to go.

Queso fresco: The most used Mexican queso in my cocina is without a doubt queso fresco. *Queso fresco* means "fresh cheese." It is mild and crumbly with a slightly salty flavor and goes well with refried beans, enchiladas, tacos dorados, and even salads.

Queso panela: Also known as *queso de canasta* because it is pressed and shaped in a corn husk–lined basket, queso panela is a fresh cheese similar in consistency to feta cheese. It is considered to be a healthier cheese option, as it is lower in fat than other quesos. This moist and creamy queso is often served in tacos placeros and salads, or atop tostadas. Panela cheese is also ideal for grilling, pan-frying, and roasting.

Requesón: Another soft, creamy cheese, requesón is similar to ricotta cheese in texture. Its mild flavor can be used in both sweet and savory dishes. Requesón is often used on its own as a filling for tamales, enchiladas, and tacos. Mixed with roasted poblano peppers or spinach, it also makes for a delicious filling for tacos dorado and flautas.

Queso Oaxaca: Similar in consistency to Italian mozzarella, this soft, mild-flavored cheese (known simply as *quesillo* in the state of Oaxaca, where it was first made) is used when making quesadillas, *chiles rellenos*, and *queso fundido*.

Queso asadero: A popular melting cheese similar to queso Oaxaca, asadero cheese is a semisoft cheese with a mild flavor ideal for nachos, *tacos de nopales asados* (grilled cactus tacos), *tacos de langosta* (lobster tacos), and my grandfather's *Chile de Rajas con Queso* (page 134).

Queso Chihuahua: This soft cheese, also known as *queso menonita* (Mennonite cheese), was first produced by the large Mennonite community in the state of Chihuahua, where it is extremely popular.

With a mild, cheddar-like flavor, this cheese is ideal to use in quesadillas, creamy soups, and *chile con queso*.

Queso añejo: This firm, aged Mexican cheese is used mostly as a garnish for tacos, enchiladas, refried beans, and tacos dorados.

Queso cotija: A firm, salty cheese popular in the state of Michoacán, where it originated, *queso cotija* is often compared to Parmesan cheese. Because it does not melt, it is best served crumbled in salads or atop grilled corn and refried beans.

Mexican crema: Not really a cheese, Mexican crema is a must-have garnish for tacos. It is similar in taste and consistency to crème fraîche, but can be a substitute for sour cream. Crema is drizzled over tostadas, enchiladas, and flautas. Or, transform it into a delicious sauce to spoon over *tacos de pescado* (fish tacos) by combining it with chiles like chipotles in adobo or fresh jalapeño. The possibilities are endless.

TUESDAY, WEDNESDAY, WHENEVER

Despite the social media popularity, tacos aren't just for Tuesdays. They are a fun and delicious meal that can be enjoyed any day of the week, and even for special occasions like a día de campo (picnic) or a summer cookout with family and friends, as well as holidays like Cinco de Mayo, Mexican Independence Day, and Día de Muertos (Day of the Dead). With so many recipes to choose from, it can be hard deciding what salsa, side dishes, and garnishes to serve with each of the main dishes. In the hopes of making things a little easier, I'm including a few menu suggestions that I often serve to my family.

QUICK & EASY WEEKNIGHT DINNER

It's been a long day and you don't want to order out, but you also don't want to spend a lot of time in the kitchen. What you need is a no-fuss meal, like my faux Tacos al Pastor (page 166), with a simple side dish and a quick and easy agua fresca.

- Tacos de Longaniza con Piña
  (Mexican longaniza tacos with pineapple; page 171)
- Refried Beans
  (page 96)
- Horchata de Avena
  (page 187)

CENA FAMILIAR (FAMILY SUPPER)

It's the weekend, and you have a little more time to plan a relaxing dinner with family. Let your slow cooker do most of the work for you.

- Carnitas *(page 45)*
- Frijoles Adobados *(page 98)*
- Calabacitas *(page 111)*
- Avocado Salsa Verde *(page 144)*
- Naranjada Mineral *(for the kiddies; page 194)*
- Clericot *(for the grown-ups; page 198)*

DÍA DE CAMPO

Grab your picnic basket and a comfy blanket, because the weather is too nice to spend the day cooped up indoors. Pack up a light meal of your favorite salads along with some tostada shells or crackers, and head out for some fresh air in the countryside, the mountains, or at your favorite park.

- Salpicón de Pollo *(chicken salpicón; page 89)*
- Ensalada de Betabel *(beet, carrot, and jicama salad; page 118)*
- Black Bean Salad w/ Corn and Nopales *(page 103)*
- Agua de Tamarindo *(tamarind agua fresca; page 189)*

CINCO DE MAYO & MEXICAN INDEPENDENCE DAY

Contrary to popular belief, Cinco de Mayo and Mexican Independence Day are not one and the same. Mexico declared its independence from Spain on September 16, 1810, while Cinco de Mayo is a celebration of Mexico's victory over the French army at the Battle of Puebla, which took place May 5, 1862. (Fun fact: Cinco de Mayo is a much bigger celebration in the United States than it is in Mexico.)

My favorite way to celebrate both of these holidays is with a good old-fashioned Mexican taquiza. Prepare a variety of your favorite taco fillings, or better yet ask your guests to bring their favorites, while you provide the side dishes, garnishes, tortillas, and beverages.

- Bistec Ranchero *(ranch-style beef; page 40)*
- Tinga de Pollo *(page 90)*
- Camarones a la Mexicana *(page 70)*
- Rajas con Crema *(page 125)*
- Chile de Molcajete *(page 132)*
- Mild Salsa Verde *(page 145)*
- Frijoles de la Olla *(page 95)*
- Arroz Mexicano *(page 100)*
- Ensalada de Nopales *(page 102)*
- Paloma *(classic tequila cocktail; page 196)*
- Piña Colada Agua Fresca *(page 195)*

SUMMER COOKOUT

Tell your guests to bring their appetite, because you will be grilling up some finger-lickin' deliciousness. This is the menu we serve most often when we head out to el rancho for a family cookout. While it is quite a lot of food, keep it budget-friendly by making it a potluck, where each of the guests brings one the items on the menu. And I speak from personal experience when I say, "Don't forget the corn tortillas!"

- Carne Asada *(page 43)*
- Cebollitas Asadas *(page 114)*
- Champiñones Rellenos Asados *(cheese-stuffed grilled mushrooms; page 116)*
- Chiles Güeros Asados con Queso *(grilled yellow peppers with cheese; page 104)*
- Nopales Asados con Queso *(grilled cactus paddles with cheese; page 122)*
- Frijoles Borrachos *(page 101)*
- Pico de Gallo *(page 139)*
- Guacamole de Molcajete *(page 137)*
- Michelada *(classic Mexican beer cocktail; page 190)*
- Agua de Jamaica *(hibiscus flower iced tea; page 188)*

DÍA DE MUERTOS

Celebrated on November 2, Día de Muertos is a Mexican holiday on which we honor our loved ones who have passed away. It's a celebration filled with bright and beautiful altars and meals shared with family and friends to remember those who are no longer with us.

- Barbacoa de Res *(page 39)*
- Poblano Rice *(page 105)*
- Agua de Guayaba *(guava agua fresca; page 193)*
- Cinnamon Buñuelos *(page 32)*
- Mexican Hot Chocolate *(page 200)*

TWO
TORTILLAS

▽ ▽

Tortillas are the cornerstone of the Mexican diet and are served with almost every meal. I consider myself lucky to live in Mexico because I have easy access to freshly made tortillas still warm from the tortillería (tortilla shop) every day. Mexican food has become much more popular worldwide over the years, and finding tortillas isn't as hard as it used to be. For those of you in the United States, tortillas are extremely popular and can be found in every supermarket. Store-bought tortillas have vastly improved in flavor and texture over the years and are great to have on hand for an easy weekday taco night.

Sin embargo (nevertheless), there is something to be said for tortillas hechas a mano, like the irresistible aroma as they cook on the comal. Homemade tortillas are softer and slightly thicker than store-bought tortillas, and their flavor is fresh and inviting. You can really savor the flavor of the ground nixtamalized corn in the masa harina used to make corn tortillas or the manteca used to make flour tortillas. Whenever I make tortillas at home, I can't help but sneak a couple of tortillas, seasoning them with only a light sprinkling of salt.

Tortillas are the base of a great tasting taco, and this chapter walks you through making great-tasting classic corn and flour tortillas in your cocina, as well as whole-wheat tortillas and chile-flavored Tortillas Rojas (page 31).

TORTILLAS

TORTILLAS DE MAÍZ

YIELD: 12 TORTILLAS   PREP TIME: 5 MINUTES   COOK TIME: 15 MINUTES

If you've ever bitten into a homemade corn tortilla and wondered how such a wonderful and distinct flavor came to be, it's all thanks to nixtamalized corn. For centuries, making corn tortillas was a long, arduous chore that included a process called nixtamalización. Nixtamalization is the process of soaking and cooking kernels of dried corn in a lime-and-water solution overnight, which softened the corn; rinsing and hulling the corn; and then finely grinding it in a metate to make masa for corn tortillas or tamales. It amazes me, given how time-consuming the process is, that Mexican mothers and grandmothers made fresh tortillas for their families daily.

While it's nice to prepare tortillas the old-fashioned way every once in a while, it has become much easier to make them these days, thanks to masa harina. Masa harina is a finely ground corn flour made from nixtamalized corn that is used to make masa for tortillas, tamales, sopes, and empanadas. You can find masa harina in the flour aisle of your local supermarket or order it online.

This recipe can easily be doubled or tripled, ensuring you always have plenty of corn tortillas on hand.

➜

TORTILLAS DE MAÍZ *continued*

2 cups masa harina
¼ teaspoon salt
1¼ cups plus 2 tablespoons
    warm water

1 Heat a comal or griddle over medium-low heat. In a large bowl, mix together the masa harina and salt. Stir in 1¼ cups of the water until the dough comes together and is smooth. If the dough is dry or crumbly, add 1 tablespoon of additional water at a time until the masa is the desired consistency.

2 Divide the dough into twelve 1½-inch balls. Using a tortilla press lined with plastic wrap or parchment paper, flatten a ball into a 6-inch circle. If you do not have a tortilla press, place a masa ball between two pieces of plastic wrap or parchment paper. Flatten with a large, heavy plate.

3 Cook a tortilla on the comal or griddle, 45 to 60 seconds per side, until fully cooked and the tortilla starts to fill with air. Remove from the heat and keep warm by covering it with a clean kitchen towel. Repeat with the remaining masa balls.

TIP *Save time in the cocina by purchasing 1 pound of ready-made tortilla masa at your local Mexican supermarket.*

TORTILLAS DE HARINA

YIELD: 12 TO 15 TORTILLAS   PREP TIME: 45 MINUTES   COOK TIME: 15 MINUTES

As much as I love corn tortillas, flour tortillas are my favorite because they are the tortillas I remember my grandmother making throughout my childhood. Flour tortillas are actually the hardest tortillas I've ever tried to make. The dough comes together quickly and easily, but rolling out perfectly round tortillas is not an easy feat. This is one instance where practice really does make perfect. The trick is to roll the dough using simple back-and-forth motions, slightly rotating the dough often.

4 cups all-purpose flour,
  plus more as needed
1 teaspoon salt
¼ teaspoon baking powder
½ cup lard or shortening
1 cup warm water, divided

1 In a large bowl, sift together the flour, salt, and baking powder. Using a pastry blender, potato masher, or two forks, cut the lard into the flour mixture until the mixture resembles coarse meal.

2 Slowly stir in ¾ cup of the water, mixing until the dough comes together and forms a ball. The dough should be soft and slightly sticky. If the dough is too dry, add 1 tablespoon of the remaining water at a time, until it is the desired consistency.

3 Knead the dough on a lightly floured surface, about 5 minutes, until smooth and elastic.

→

4 Return the dough to the bowl; cover with plastic wrap and let rest for 30 minutes.

5 Heat a comal or griddle over medium heat.

6 Divide the dough into twelve to fifteen 1½- to 2-inch balls. Using the palm of your hand, flatten each ball gently on a lightly floured surface. Sprinkle each ball of dough lightly with flour. Using a rolling pin, roll a dough ball into an oval shape. Rotate the dough slightly; roll back and forth with the rolling pin. Continue rotating and rolling solely back and forth until you've formed an 8- to 10-inch circle.

7 Cook the tortillas on the comal for about 30 seconds per side, until the tortilla starts to fill with air. Remove from the heat and keep warm by covering it with a clean kitchen towel. Repeat with the remaining balls of dough.

TIP *Keep your tortillas in an air-tight container for up to a week. Before using, warm them either on a skillet or comal, or in the microwave for a few seconds.*

WHOLE-WHEAT FLOUR TORTILLAS

YIELD: 12 TO 15 TORTILLAS   PREP TIME: 45 MINUTES   COOK TIME: 15 MINUTES

Whole-wheat tortillas are a healthier tortilla alternative to flour tortillas made with lard and are a tasty way to incorporate more whole grains in your diet. Making them at home is easy and results in better tasting tortillas than store-bought ones. They are perfect to use for quesadillas, tacos, or even wraps. I like to use whole-wheat tortillas as a substitute for pita bread in tacos Árabes (see Tacos al Pastor, page 166).

2½ cups whole-wheat flour
1½ cups all-purpose flour
1 teaspoon salt
¼ teaspoon baking powder
½ cup shortening
1½ cups very warm
  water, divided

1 In a large bowl, sift together the whole-wheat flour, all-purpose flour, salt, and baking powder. Using a pastry blender, potato masher, or two forks, cut the shortening into the flour until the mixture resembles coarse meal. Slowly stir in 1 cup of the warm water, mixing until dough comes together and forms a ball. The dough should be soft and slightly sticky. If dough is too dry, add 1 tablespoon of the remaining water at a time, until it is the desired consistency.

2 On a lightly floured surface, knead the dough about 5 minutes, until smooth and elastic. Return the dough to the bowl; cover with plastic wrap and let rest for 30 minutes.

3 Heat a comal or griddle over medium heat.

➤

4 Divide the dough into twelve to fifteen 1½- to 2-inch balls. On a lightly floured surface, flatten each ball of dough lightly with the palm of your hand. Sprinkle each ball of dough lightly with flour. Using a rolling pin, roll a ball of dough into an oval shape. Rotate the dough slightly; roll back and forth with the rolling pin. Continue rotating and rolling solely back and forth until you've formed an 8- to 10-inch circle.

5 Cook the tortilla on the warm comal for about 30 seconds per side, until it starts to fill with air. Remove from the heat and keep warm by covering it with a clean kitchen towel. Repeat with the remaining balls of dough.

TIP *To store the tortillas, let them cool completely before storing in a clean plastic storage bag. The tortillas will keep for about a week.*

TORTILLAS ROJAS

YIELD: 12 TORTILLAS   PREP TIME: 15 MINUTES   COOK TIME: 15 MINUTES

Popular in the northern region of Mexico, these vibrant corn tortillas are flavored with dried ancho and guajillo chiles. I prefer to prepare my tortillas rojas with chicken broth for an added level of flavor, but water will work just as well. Traditionally, these tortillas are used to make enchiladas, quesadillas, and, of course, tacos, but my favorite way to pair them is with Rajas con Crema (page 125) or Refried Beans (page 96) topped with lots of shredded queso Oaxaca.

1½ cups chicken broth
   or water
1 dried ancho chile,
   stemmed and seeded
1 dried guajillo chile,
   stemmed and seeded
2 cups masa harina
¼ teaspoon salt

TIP Change the flavor of your Tortillas Rojas by substituting the dried ancho chile with dried pasilla chiles or dried chipotles.

1 In a medium saucepan over high heat, bring the chicken broth and dried chiles to a boil. Remove from the heat. Cover the saucepan to allow chiles to soften; let cool completely. Purée the chiles and broth in a blender until smooth.

2 Preheat a comal or griddle over medium heat.

3 In a medium bowl, combine the masa harina and salt. Stir in the chile purée, mixing until the dough comes together and forms a ball.

4 Divide the dough into twelve 1½-inch balls. Using a tortilla press lined with two pieces of plastic wrap or parchment paper, flatten a ball of masa into a 6-inch circle. If you do not have a tortilla press, place a masa ball between two pieces of plastic wrap or parchment paper. Flatten with a large, heavy plate.

5 Cook the tortilla on the comal or griddle for 45 to 60 seconds per side, until fully cooked and the tortilla starts to fill with air. Remove from the heat and keep warm by covering it with a clean kitchen towel. Repeat with the remaining masa balls.

CINNAMON BUÑUELOS

YIELD: 12 TO 15 BUÑUELOS   PREP TIME: 45 MINUTES   COOK TIME: 15 MINUTES

Flour tortillas aren't just for burritos, quesadillas, and tacos. The same masa used to make flour tortillas can also be used to make cinnamon buñuelos. Crispy, fried flour tortillas topped with granulated sugar and ground cinnamon are a sweet treat that both kiddies and grown-ups can't resist. My grandparents would make dozens of cinnamon buñuelos to share with family, friends, and neighbors for Thanksgiving and Christmas. You can enjoy this traditional Mexican dessert anytime of the year.

1 batch *Tortillas de Harina* masa (flour tortilla dough, page 27)
2 cups vegetable oil, for frying
All-purpose flour, for dusting
1½ cups granulated sugar
1 tablespoon ground cinnamon

TIP *Save time in the cocina by using store-bought flour or whole-wheat tortillas.*

1 Prepare flour tortilla masa according to *Tortillas de Harina* instructions on page 27 just until you knead the dough. Shape dough into 1½- to 2-inch balls. Return the balls of masa to the bowl; cover with plastic wrap and let rest for 30 minutes.

2 On a lightly floured surface, flatten each ball of dough gently with the palm of your hand. Sprinkle each ball of dough lightly with flour. Using a rolling pin, roll the dough into an oval shape. Rotate the dough slightly; roll back and forth with the rolling pin. Continue rotating and rolling slowly back and forth until you've formed a 10-inch circle.

3 In a large skillet, heat the oil over medium-high heat. Fry each tortilla for 1½ to 2 minutes per side, until golden and crisp. Transfer fried tortillas to a paper towel–lined plate to drain any excess oil. Repeat with the remaining tortillas.

4 In a large bowl, combine the granulated sugar with the ground cinnamon. Dip the warm tortillas in the cinnamon-sugar mixture until completely coated on both sides.

5 Enjoy *Cinnamon Buñuelos* with a cup of *Mexican Hot Chocolate* (page 200).

TACOS, TAQUITOS, FLAUTAS & BURRITOS

An important lesson for taco enthusiasts is learning the difference between tacos, taquitos, flautas, and burritos. All four use a tortilla base, which may lead to the misunderstanding that all Mexican food is the same, but each is prepared and served in its own unique way.

Tacos are primarily made using corn tortillas, though flour tortillas are sometimes used, especially in the northern region of Mexico. Tacos are topped with filling, garnish, and/or salsa, then folded in half to prevent the filling from falling out while lifting to eat.

Taquito means "little taco," which is a misnomer because taquitos aren't miniature versions of tacos. A taquito is a corn tortilla tightly rolled around its filling. Taquitos are fried in oil to a golden crisp. Traditionally, taquitos are served topped with shredded lettuce or cabbage, guacamole, salsa, or Mexican crema, with a sprinkling of crumbled queso fresco or queso cotija (two types of Mexican cheese) on top.

Flautas, made with flour tortillas or two overlapping corn tortillas, are also a rolled, fried, stuffed tortilla, but they tend to be longer than taquitos, similar to a flute (flauta is the Spanish word for "flute"). Although there is a slight difference between both flautas and taquitos, the terms are often used interchangeably.

A **burrito** can be made with practically every kind of filling imaginable, whether it's just a simple carne asada or a combination of a meat guisado with beans, rice, and guacamole. The ends of the tortilla are tucked in to help contain the filling, and then the tortilla is wrapped around the filling like an envelope forming a package of deliciousness.

THREE
BEEF, PORK & MORE

▽▽▽▽▽▽▽▽▽▽ ▽▽▽▽▽▽ ▽ ▽ ▽▽▽▽▽▽ ▽ ▽ ▽▽▽▽

This chapter is a meat lover's delight! It's packed with sizzling grilled meats and tasty guisados made mostly with beef and pork, but adventurous eaters will appreciate that I've included a couple of recipes made with lamb and goat. All of the recipes in this chapter can be served on their own with your choice of sides (I've included a couple of suggestions) and as filling for tacos, burritos, tortas (Mexican sandwiches), or quesadillas.

This chapter offers a little bit of everything, from comforting classics like Chile Colorado *(page 46),* Bistec Ranchero *(page 40),* Asado de Res *(page 38), and* Queso Fundido *(page 57) to grilled favorites like* Carne Asada *(made with skirt steak; page 43) and* Carne Enchilada *(page 44).*

BEEF, PORK & MORE

ALAMBRES DE ARRACHERA

YIELD: 6 SERVINGS   PREP TIME: 30 MINUTES   COOK TIME: 20 MINUTES

Considering this dish consists of thin strips of meat sautéed with onions and fresh chile peppers (or bell peppers) all covered in melted cheese, it's no wonder alambres are a popular dish throughout Mexico. Alambres can be made with beef, pork, or chicken. I prefer arrachera *(skirt steak) because it is tender, moist, and full of flavor and cooks up quickly. Serve with warm tortillas,* Nopales Asados con Queso *(page 122),* Refried Beans *(page 96), and* Chile de Molcajete *(page 132).*

1½ to 2 pounds skirt steak, cut into thin strips

2 tablespoons Maggi Jugo Seasoning Sauce or Worcestershire sauce

2 tablespoons vegetable oil, divided

Coarse salt

Freshly ground black pepper

6 banana peppers, seeded and cut into thin strips

½ medium onion, thinly sliced

2 garlic cloves, minced

1½ cups shredded queso asadero

1 In an 8-inch square baking dish, place the steak and sprinkle the Maggi Jugo over the meat, turning to coat. Cover with plastic wrap and refrigerate for at least 30 minutes.

2 In a grill pan, heat 1 tablespoon of the oil over high heat. Add the skirt steak and cook for 3 to 5 minutes, until nice and brown. Turn the strips over, season with salt and pepper, and cook for 3 to 5 minutes more, to desired doneness. Remove from the heat and cover with aluminum foil for 5 minutes.

3 In a large nonstick skillet, heat the remaining 1 tablespoon of the oil over high heat. Sauté the banana peppers and onion for 2 to 3 minutes, until the onion is translucent. Season lightly with salt. Stir in the garlic and cooked skirt steak and sauté for 1 to 2 minutes more. Remove from the heat. Sprinkle the asadero cheese over.

TIP *You can use Monterrey Jack or provolone cheese if you can't find asadero. Also, for added flavor, add 2 ounces of your favorite tequila to the marinade.*

ASADO DE RES A LA CERVEZA

YIELD: 6 TO 8 SERVINGS   PREP TIME: 30 MINUTES   COOK TIME: 2½ HOURS

Asado de Res *is a delicious meat roast flavored with Mexican lager, which helps tenderize the meat into juicy, mouthwatering pieces. The beer, Maggi Jugo, and Worcestershire serve as incredible flavor enhancers, while the spices that are added once the meat is done roasting kick things up a notch. Grab a stack of warm flour tortillas, a few lime wedges, and your favorite spicy, Mexican salsa. For a complete meal, serve with* Refried Beans *(page 96) and* Poblano Rice *(page 105).*

3 tablespoons oil, divided

2½- to 3-pound tri-tip roast, cut into 3-inch pieces

1 medium onion, thinly sliced

3 garlic cloves, minced

¼ cup lime juice

1 (12-ounce) bottle dark or lager Mexican beer

1 tablespoon Maggi Jugo Seasoning Sauce

1 tablespoon Worcestershire sauce

1½ teaspoons coarse salt

1 teaspoon freshly ground black pepper

1 teaspoon ground cumin

1 teaspoon crushed Mexican oregano

Flour tortillas, for serving

Chile de Rajas con Queso (page 134)

Cebollitas Asadas (page 114)

1 Preheat the oven to 425°F.

2 In a Dutch oven or large heat-proof saucepan, heat 2 tablespoons of the oil over high heat. Working in batches if necessary, sear the meat, 5 to 6 minutes per side, until lightly browned. Transfer the meat to a heat-proof plate.

3 Add the remaining 1 tablespoon of the oil and sauté the onion for 2 to 3 minutes, until translucent. Add the garlic and sauté for an additional 30 seconds. Stir in the lime juice, scraping the bottom of the pan to deglaze. Add the beer, Maggi Jugo, Worcestershire sauce, salt, pepper, cumin, and oregano. Return the meat to the pan and bring to a boil over high heat. Remove from the heat.

4 Cover and bake for 1 hour. Reduce the heat to 350°F and continue to bake for 45 minutes. Remove from the oven and shred the meat with two forks. Return the pan to oven and bake uncovered for 15 minutes more.

5 Serve with flour tortillas, *Chile de Rajas con Queso,* and *Cebollitas Asadas.*

BARBACOA DE RES

DAIRY FREE

YIELD: 6 TO 8 SERVINGS   PREP TIME: 10 MINUTES   COOK TIME: 6 TO 8 HOURS

Before retiring, Pappy (my grandfather) always took over the kitchen on weekends and holidays. One of Pappy's preferred methods of cooking was using his trusty slow cooker to create many traditional Mexican dishes, like his signature pork Chile Colorado *(page 46) and this barbacoa de res. I have fond memories of both dishes, and I make sure to always add plenty of garlic and cumin—Pappy's favorite spices—for a truly comforting meal that reminds me of my childhood.*

4 roma tomatoes

2 dried guajillo chiles, stemmed and seeded

2 dried pasilla chiles, stemmed and seeded

3 cups water

2 garlic cloves

½ medium white onion, chopped, plus more for garnish

1 teaspoon ground cumin

½ teaspoon dried oregano, crushed

Coarse salt

Cooking spray

4 to 5 pounds beef shanks or boneless country-style beef ribs

Freshly ground black pepper

2 bay leaves

Chopped cilantro (for garnish)

Warm corn or flour tortillas

1 In a medium saucepan, bring the tomatoes, dried chiles, and water to a boil over high heat. Cover, reduce the heat to low, and simmer for 8 to 10 minutes or until the tomatoes are cooked through. Remove from the heat and cool slightly.

2 In a blender, add the cooked tomatoes, dried chiles, their cooking water, the garlic, and the onion and blend until smooth. Stir in the cumin and oregano and season with salt.

3 Lightly grease the inside of a slow cooker with cooking spray. Season the beef shanks with salt and pepper. Arrange the shanks in the slow cooker and pour the chile purée over. Place the bay leaves on top of the purée. Cover and cook on the low-heat setting for 6 to 8 hours.

4 Ladle the barbacoa de res into bowls. Garnish with chopped white onion and cilantro. Serve with warm corn or flour tortillas.

TIP For a hearty stew, add 3 medium potatoes and 4 medium carrots—peeled and cut into bite-size pieces—to the slow cooker.

BISTEC RANCHERO

YIELD: 6 TO 8 SERVINGS   PREP TIME: 10 MINUTES   COOK TIME: 45 MINUTES

Thin strips of beef simmered in a simple tomato broth with potatoes, carrots, onions, and bell peppers make for a hearty and comforting guisado. When served on its own, top with cooked nopales and servings of Sopa de Fideo Seco *(page 106) and* Chile de Molcajete *(page 132) on the side.*

FOR THE PURÉE

3 whole roma tomatoes
½ medium white onion
1 garlic clove
2½ cups water

FOR THE BEEF

1 tablespoon vegetable oil
½ medium white onion,
   finely chopped
2 green bell peppers,
   seeded and diced
2 serrano chiles, seeded
   and finely chopped
2 garlic cloves, minced
1½ pounds thin-cut steak,
   cut into thin strips
3 roma tomatoes, diced
2 medium potatoes,
   peeled and diced
2 medium carrots, peeled
   and thinly sliced
Cilantro sprigs
1 teaspoon coarse salt
½ teaspoon black pepper

TO MAKE THE PURÉE

In a blender, purée the tomatoes, onion, garlic, and water until smooth.

TO MAKE THE BEEF

1 In a Dutch oven or large nonstick skillet, heat the oil over high heat. Add the onion, bell peppers, and serrano chiles and sauté for 2 to 3 minutes, until the onion is translucent.

2 Add the garlic and sauté for an additional 30 seconds. Add the meat and sauté for 5 to 8 minutes, until cooked through.

3 Stir in the tomatoes, potatoes, carrots, tomato purée, and a few cilantro sprigs. Season with the salt and pepper. As soon as the guisado starts to boil, reduce the heat to low. Cover and simmer for 20 to 25 minutes, until the meat and vegetables are tender.

TIP *Substitute ground chicken or turkey for the thin-cut steak for a comforting picadillo ranchero (ranch-style picadillo).*

CABRITO ASADO

YIELD: 6 TO 8 SERVINGS   PREP TIME: 30 MINUTES   COOK TIME: 6 TO 8 HOURS

If you've ever come across goat at the supermarket and wondered what to make with it, I suggest you try this recipe. The official dish of the state of Nuevo León, roasted goat is traditionally slow roasted over an open flame. This slow cooker version is a great starting point for anyone who has never tried this hearty and flavorful meat, with a bit of gaminess. Don't worry, though, because the citrus juices not only tenderize the meat, but they tone down that gamey flavor.

Cooking spray
1 large onion, thinly sliced, divided
2 to 3 tablespoons vegetable oil
2½ pounds boneless goat, cut into 2-inch pieces
2 cups fresh orange juice
¼ cup freshly squeezed lime juice
Salt
Freshly ground black pepper
1 teaspoon crushed Mexican oregano
2 garlic cloves, minced
1 teaspoon dried rosemary, lightly crushed
1 teaspoon of dried thyme, lightly crushed
Handful cilantro leaves
Flour tortillas, warmed, for serving
Lime wedges, for serving
Salsa, for serving

1 Lightly coat the inside of a slow cooker with cooking spray. Arrange half of the onion slices in the bottom of the slow cooker.

2 In a large nonstick skillet, heat 2 tablespoons of the oil over high heat. Add the goat meat and sear, working in batches if necessary, for 12 to 15 minutes, until golden brown on all sides. Remove from the heat and transfer the meat to the slow cooker, arranging it on top of the onion slices.

3 In the slow cooker, pour the orange and lime juices over the meat, then season with salt, pepper, and oregano. Top with the remaining sliced onion, garlic, rosemary, thyme, and cilantro. Cover and cook on the low-heat setting for 6 to 8 hours, or until the meat is easily shredded.

4 Serve with warm flour tortillas, lime wedges, and your favorite salsa.

TIP *The best cuts of goat meat for slow roasting are the shoulder and back. A younger goat (kid) results in a tender and mild-flavored roast, while an older goat (nanny) results in a slightly tougher roast with a stronger flavor. A nanny goat will require the full 8 hours of cooking time.*

BEEF, PORK & MORE

41

CARNE ADOBADA

YIELD: 8 SERVINGS   PREP TIME: 3 HOURS 20 MINUTES   COOK TIME: 30 MINUTES

Making tacos de adobada is easy here in Mexico because most carnicerías (butcher shops) sell finely chopped pieces of pork in a spicy marinade. Each carnicero (butcher) makes their own unique adobo—which not only adds tons of flavor, but also helps tenderize the meat—that ranges from mild to super spicy. But making this filling at home is easy, especially because you control the meat quality and the amount of chiles and spices.

3 dried ancho chiles, stemmed and seeded
3 dried guajillo chiles, stemmed and seeded
3 dried pasilla chiles, stemmed and seeded
3 cups water
2 garlic cloves
½ medium onion
1 cup white vinegar
1½ teaspoons coarse salt
1 teaspoon ground cumin
½ teaspoon freshly ground black pepper
½ teaspoon dried oregano
¼ teaspoon ground cinnamon
2 pounds pork shoulder roast, finely chopped
2 tablespoons vegetable oil
Refried Beans (page 96)
Poblano Rice (page 105)

1 In a medium saucepan, bring the dried chiles and water to a boil over high heat. Cover, reduce the heat to low, and simmer for about 5 minutes, until the chiles have softened. Remove from the heat and cool to room temperature. Drain.

2 Blend the softened chiles, garlic, onion, vinegar, salt, cumin, pepper, oregano, and cinnamon in a blender until smooth.

3 In a large bowl or baking dish, mix together the pork and chile purée until the meat is coated. Cover with plastic wrap and refrigerate for at least 3 hours and up to overnight.

4 In a large skillet, heat the oil over high heat. Add the carne adobada and cook for 10 to 15 minutes, until the meat is cooked through. Cover, reduce the heat to low, and simmer, stirring occasionally, for 12 to 15 minutes, until all of the juices from the meat and adobo sauce have evaporated and the meat has started to brown. Serve with *Refried Beans* and *Poblano Rice*, or use as a filling for tacos.

TIP *If dried pasilla chiles aren't available, increase the number of dried ancho chiles to 6. Also, you can substitute one (14-ounce) can mild enchilada sauce for the dried chiles and water.*

CARNE ASADA

Carne asada, or "grilled meat," refers to any cut of beef (thick or thin) cooked on the grill, comal, or plancha. The term carne asada can also refer to a cookout/barbecue, as in "I'm hosting a carne asada this weekend; you bring the tequila!" Arrachera is my favorite cut of meat to grill, and marinating it in a flavorful mixture of cerveza (beer), lime juice, garlic, and black pepper gives it a tangy, hoppy pepperiness.

1 (12-ounce) bottle dark Mexican beer

¼ cup freshly squeezed lime juice

3 garlic cloves, minced

2 teaspoons Worcestershire sauce

1 teaspoon Maggi Jugo Seasoning Sauce

1 teaspoon freshly ground black pepper

½ teaspoon salt

½ teaspoon ground cumin

2 pounds arrachera (skirt steak)

1 tablespoon vegetable oil (if grilling in a grill pan)

Champiñones Rellenos Asados (page 116)

Cebollitas Asadas (page 114)

Chiles Güeros Asados con Queso (page 104)

Corn tortillas, for serving

1 In a a 9x13-inch baking dish, mix the beer, lime juice, garlic, Worcestershire sauce, Maggi Jugo, pepper, salt, and cumin. Add the arrachera to the marinade and turn to coat. Cover with plastic wrap and marinate in the refrigerator for at least 3 hours.

2 Preheat the grill to medium.

3 Grill the arrachera for 7 to 10 minutes per side (for medium-rare to medium), or to desired doneness. To prepare the carne asada on the stove top, heat the oil in a grill pan over medium-high heat. Cook the arrachera for 8 to 10 minutes per side to desired doneness.

4 Transfer the carne asada to a platter. Cover with a sheet of aluminum foil and rest for 5 minutes before serving. Slice into thin strips.

5 Serve carne asada with grilled sides like Champiñones Rellenos Asados, Cebollitas Asadas, and Chiles Güeros Asados con Queso, and plenty of corn tortillas.

TIP If you are serving the carne asada as a filling for tacos or burritos, roughly chop the cooked arrachera into bite-size pieces.

CARNE ENCHILADA DE RES

YIELD: 4 TO 6 SERVINGS   PREP TIME: 3 HOURS 15 MINUTES   COOK TIME: 20 MINUTES

You might be thinking that Carne Enchilada *is Spanish for a beef-filled enchilada, but it's not. Carne enchilada is chile-marinated steak that is pan-fried or grilled. It's delicious served with flour tortillas, refried beans, grilled nopales, and a crisp salad. Or slice it into thin strips for a taco filling and top with* Ensalada de Nopales *(page 102) and* Guacamole de Molcajete *(page 137). My grandfather loved having carne enchilada for breakfast with a fried egg on top.*

3 dried ancho chiles

3 dried guajillo chiles

3 cups water

2 garlic cloves, minced

¼ medium white onion, chopped

1½ teaspoons salt, plus more for seasoning

½ teaspoon freshly ground black pepper

½ teaspoon ground cinnamon

½ teaspoon ground cumin

½ teaspoon crushed Mexican oregano

2 tablespoons white vinegar

1½ pounds thin-cut top round steaks

1 tablespoon vegetable oil

Warm flour tortillas, for serving

Arroz Mexicano (page 100)

Refried Beans (page 96)

Ensalada de Nopales (page 102)

1 In a medium saucepan, bring the dried chiles and water to a boil over medium-high heat. Cover, reduce the heat to low, and simmer for about 5 minutes, until the chiles have softened. Remove from the heat and cool slightly.

2 Blend the softened chiles, ½ cup of the cooking water, garlic, onion, salt, pepper, cinnamon, cumin, oregano, and vinegar in a blender until smooth.

3 In a 9x13-inch baking dish, place the meat and pour the adobo sauce over it, making sure the meat is completely submerged. Cover with plastic wrap and refrigerate for at least 3 hours.

4 In a grill pan or large nonstick skillet, heat the oil over medium-high heat. Cook 2 to 3 steaks at a time, for 5 to 7 minutes per side to desired doneness, seasoning lightly with salt after flipping, if desired.

5 Serve with warm flour tortillas, *Arroz Mexicano*, *Refried Beans*, and *Ensalada de Nopales*.

TIP *You can also grill* Carne Enchilada *over a medium flame to desired doneness for a divine smoky version.*

CARNITAS

One of the tastiest foods I discovered soon after moving to Mexico was carnitas, which means "little meats." My first encounter with these beautifully golden fried meat pieces was at a family get-together. I had no idea what they were, but I knew I wanted them. It was love at first taste, and now carnitas are my go-to recipe for when I need to feed a crowd.

Traditionally carnitas are slow cooked in manteca *or* manteca de cerdo *(pork lard) in a large copper* cazo *(pot) over a wood-burning fire until golden and crisp on the outside, but tender and juicy on the inside. Done right, carnitas are melt-in-your-mouth tasty goodness.*

Cooking spray

2 to 4 tablespoons manteca de cerdo

2¼ pounds pork shoulder roast or Boston butt, cut into 2- to 3-inch pieces

1½ teaspoons salt

1 teaspoon ground cumin

½ teaspoon freshly ground black pepper

1 cup orange juice

½ cup freshly squeezed lime juice

2 bay leaves

Cilantro sprigs

Frijoles Borrachos (page 101)

Arroz Mexicano (page 100)

Chiles Torreados (page 135)

1 Grease the inside of a slow cooker with cooking spray.

2 In a large skillet, heat 2 tablespoons of the manteca over high heat. Add the roast and sear on all sides, adding more lard if necessary, for 10 to 12 minutes, until lightly browned. Remove from the heat and transfer to the slow cooker.

3 In a medium bowl, whisk together the salt, cumin, pepper, and orange and lime juices. Pour the mixture over the roast. Top the roast with the bay leaves and cilantro sprigs. Cover and cook on the low-heat setting for 6 to 8 hours. Serve with *Frijoles Borrachos, Arroz Mexicano,* and *Chiles Torreados.*

TIP *If you are using the carnitas as a filling for tacos or tortas, shred with 2 forks.*

BEEF, PORK & MORE

CHILE COLORADO

YIELD: 6 TO 8 SERVINGS PREP TIME: 20 MINUTES COOK TIME: 6 TO 8 HOURS

This was my abuelito's (grandpa's) signature dish that he loved to make every chance he got. Pappy was born and raised in the state of Chihuahua, where Chile Colorado—which can be made with beef, pork, or machaca (dried beef)—is one of the state's official dishes. When I was growing up, dried chiles were hard to come by, so Pappy always used canned enchilada sauce, but I've adapted his recipe by making my own sauce with dried ancho and guajillo chiles.

4 dried ancho chiles, stemmed and seeded

2 dried guajillo chiles, stemmed and seeded

4 cups water

3 garlic cloves

¼ cup masa harina

1½ teaspoons coarse salt, divided

Cooking spray

2¼ pounds pork loin or pork stew meat, cut into 1-inch chunks

¾ teaspoon freshly ground black pepper

1 teaspoon ground cumin

½ teaspoon crushed oregano

1 medium onion, sliced

6 cilantro sprigs

2 cups cooked nopales (see step 1 of *Ensalada de Nopales*, page 102, for technique)

2 cups cooked pinto beans

1 In a medium saucepan, bring the dried chiles and water to a boil over high heat. Cover, reduce the heat to low, and simmer for 5 minutes, until the chiles have softened. Remove from the heat and cool slightly.

2 Blend the chiles and their water, the garlic, masa harina, and ¾ teaspoon of the salt in a blender until smooth.

3 Lightly grease the inside of a slow cooker with cooking spray. Put the pork in the slow cooker and season with the remaining ¾ teaspoon of the salt, the pepper, cumin, and oregano. Top with the onion and cilantro. Pour the chile purée over the pork. Cover and cook on the low-heat setting for 6 to 8 hours, until meat is tender. Serve with nopales and pinto beans.

TIP Save time in the cocina by substituting 1 (28-ounce) can of red enchilada sauce (mild or hot) for the sauce.

CHILORIO

YIELD: 4 TO 6 SERVINGS   PREP TIME: 15 MINUTES   COOK TIME: 30 MINUTES

Chilorio is a seasoned shredded pork filling for tacos, quesadillas, tostadas, and tortas. It's such a versatile filling that it is even sold canned, like tuna. Traditionally the pork meat is simmered in a mixture of water, manteca, and spices, before adding the dried chile adobo, but I rarely ever prepare it completely from scratch. I prefer to use leftover shredded pork roast or carnitas to make a quick and easy chilorio that I can serve for breakfast, lunch, or dinner.

3 dried pasilla chiles,
  stemmed and seeded
2 dried guajillo chiles,
  stemmed and seeded
3 cups water
2 garlic cloves
2 tablespoons white vinegar
Salt
2 tablespoons manteca or
  vegetable oil
3 cups cooked shredded
  pork, such as leftover
  carnitas or pork roast
½ teaspoon crushed
  Mexican oregano
½ teaspoon ground cumin
Warm flour tortillas,
  for serving
Chopped white onion,
  for garnish
Diced avocado, for garnish

1 In a medium saucepan, bring the dried chiles and water to a boil over high heat. Cover, reduce the heat to low, and simmer for 5 minutes, until the chiles have softened. Remove from the heat and cool slightly.

2 Blend the chiles and their cooking water, the garlic, and the vinegar in a blender until smooth. Season with salt.

3 In a large nonstick skillet, heat the manteca over medium-high heat. Add the shredded pork and cook for 8 to 10 minutes, until the meat starts to brown. Pour the chile purée over the pork. Stir in the oregano and cumin. Cover, reduce the heat to low, and simmer for 10 to 15 minutes to allow the flavors to develop.

4 Serve with warm flour tortillas and garnish with chopped white onion and diced avocado.

TIP *Add 2 peeled and diced medium potatoes to the meat while simmering for a heartier dish.*

COSTILLITAS EN SALSA VERDE

YIELD: 6 TO 8 SERVINGS PREP TIME: 1 HOUR COOK TIME: 1 HOUR 40 MINUTES

This recipe was one of the first meals my husband cooked for me when we were newlyweds, and it continues to be one of his all-time favorite meals. Carnicerías in Mexico almost always cut ribs crosswise instead of lengthwise, unless specially ordered, so that they can be simmered in moles, soups, stews, and guisados.

FOR THE SALSA VERDE

2 pounds tomatillos, husks removed
4 to 6 serrano chiles
4 cups water
¼ medium onion
1 garlic clove
Handful cilantro leaves
1 teaspoon coarse salt

TO MAKE THE SALSA VERDE

1 In a medium pot, bring the tomatillos, chiles, and water to a boil over medium-high heat. Cover, reduce the heat to low, and simmer for about 15 minutes until tomatillos are cooked through. Remove from the heat and cool slightly.

2 Blend the tomatillos and their cooking water, onion, garlic, and cilantro in a blender until smooth. Season with the salt. Set aside.

FOR THE RIBS

2 pounds cross-cut pork spareribs, cut into individual pieces

1 medium onion, cut into quarters

2 garlic cloves, minced

Handful cilantro leaves

1 teaspoon coarse salt

2 tablespoons vegetable oil

4 medium potatoes, peeled and diced

Warm tortillas, for serving

Cooked nopales (see step 1 of *Ensalada de Nopales*, page 102, for technique)

Sopa de Fideo Seco (page 106)

TO MAKE THE RIBS

1 In a Dutch oven or large saucepan, place the spare ribs, onion, garlic, and cilantro. Fill the Dutch oven with enough water to completely cover the ribs. Add the salt and bring to a boil over high heat, skimming off any foam that rises to the top. Cover, reduce the heat to low, and simmer for 45 minutes to 1 hour until the ribs are tender. Remove the ribs and discard the remaining solids and liquids.

2 Return the ribs to the pot and heat over medium-high heat. Add the oil and cook, for 10 to 12 minutes, until evenly browned all over. Stir in the salsa verde and potatoes and season with salt, if necessary. When the salsa verde starts to boil, cover, reduce the heat to low, and simmer for 20 to 25 minutes.

3 Ladle into bowls. Serve with warm tortillas, cooked nopales, and *Sopa de Fideo Seco*.

TIP *Change the flavor completely by switching up the salsas. Try* Chile de Molcajete *(page 132) and* Salsa de Chile Guajillo *(page 141).*

DISCADA

YIELD: 6 TO 8 SERVINGS   PREP TIME: 15 MINUTES   COOK TIME: 45 MINUTES

Traditionally discadas are prepared in a large disco (plow disc)—also known as a cowboy wok—over an open flame. Discadas are a meat lover's dream, with a little bit of everything from bacon to boneless pork chops to thin-cut steak and even Mexican chorizo mixed in. An easily doubled, or even tripled, recipe, this is perfect for feeding a crowd. Serve with Refried Beans *(page 96),* Guacamole de Molcajete *(page 137),* Chiles Torreados *(page 135), and lime wedges.*

1 tablespoon vegetable oil

6 bacon slices, cut into 1-inch pieces

2 boneless pork chops, chopped

6 ounces thin-cut steak, cut into strips

6 ounces Mexican *Pork Chorizo* (page 56), sliced

4 to 6 hot dogs, sliced

6 ounces deli ham, chopped

1 medium onion, sliced

2 green bell peppers, cut into thin matchsticks

3 serrano chiles, seeded and finely chopped

4 tomatoes, chopped

3 garlic cloves, minced

1 (12-ounce) bottle dark or lager Mexican beer

1 (16-ounce) bottle Clamato

1 tablespoon Worcestershire sauce

1 tablespoon Maggi Jugo Seasoning Sauce

Salt

Freshly ground black pepper

Refried Beans (page 96)

Guacamole de Molcajete (page 137)

Chiles Torreados (page 135)

Lime wedges, for serving

1 In a Dutch oven or large skillet, heat the oil over high heat. Add the bacon and cook, stirring occasionally, for about 3 minutes, until browned but not completely crisp. Transfer the bacon to a paper towel–lined plate.

2 Add the pork chops and cook, stirring occasionally, for 8 to 10 minutes, until lightly browned. Stir in the steak strips and cook for 5 to 7 minutes, until no longer pink. Add the chorizo, hot dogs, and ham, and cook for 8 to 10 minutes, until the chorizo is fully cooked.

3 Stir in the onion, bell pepper, chiles, tomatoes, and garlic, and cook, stirring occasionally, for 3 to 5 minutes, until the onion turns tranluscent.

4 Pour in the beer, Clamato, Worcestershire sauce, and Maggi Jugo. Season with salt and pepper. Cover and simmer for 15 to 20 minutes, until the beer has almost completely evaporated.

5 Serve with *Refried Beans, Guacamole de Molcajete, Chiles Torreados,* and lime wedges.

TIP *For a more filling dish, stir in 2 cups cooked nopales and 2 cups cooked beans with the beer.*

COCHINITA PIBIL

Tender pieces of marinated pork wrapped in banana leaves and slow roasted for hours until the meat practically melts in your mouth, Cochinita Pibil is a traditional Mexican dish from the Yucatán peninsula. With fresh banana leaves and achiote paste readily available in supermarkets and online, and with the help of your slow cooker, you, too, can now enjoy this Mexican delicacy at home. Don't worry if you can't find banana leaves; this recipe is still delicious without them.

Cooking spray
1 to 2 banana leaves, divided
1 (3.5-ounce) packet
  achiote paste
1¼ cup orange juice
½ cup lime juice
¼ cup white vinegar
3 garlic cloves
1 teaspoon coarse salt, plus
  more for seasoning
1 teaspoon ground cumin
½ teaspoon freshly ground
  black pepper, plus more
  for seasoning
½ teaspoon ground
  cinnamon
½ teaspoon dried Mexican
  oregano, crushed
½ medium onion, sliced
2 pounds pork shoulder
  roast or Boston butt, cut
  into 3-inch pieces
Refried Beans (page 96)
Cebollas Encurtidas
  (page 131)

1 Lightly grease the inside of a slow cooker with cooking spray.

2 Heat a comal or griddle over medium-high heat. Warm the banana leaves on the hot comal, turning occasionally, for 2 to 3 minutes, just until soft and pliable. Remove from the heat. Arrange the banana leaves inside the slow cooker to cover the bottom, cutting as necessary.

3 Blend the achiote paste, orange and lime juices, vinegar, garlic, salt, cumin, pepper, cinnamon, and oregano in a blender until smooth.

4 Season the pork lightly with salt and pepper. Place the pork inside the banana leaf–lined slow cooker. Pour the chile purée over the pork meat. Top with the sliced onion. Cover the pork with another banana leaf.

5 Cook on the low-heat setting for 6 to 8 hours, until the pork is tender. Using two forks, shred the pork. Serve with *Refried Beans* and garnish with *Cebollas Encurtidas.*

TIP *Achiote paste tends to stain, so rinse your blender cup with cold water immediately.*

GROUND BEEF PICADILLO

YIELD: 6 SERVINGS   PREP TIME: 15 MINUTES   COOK TIME: 40 MINUTES

When I was growing up, ground beef picadillo was one of the comforting dishes in my grandparents' weekly dinner rotation. This picadillo combines elements of both my grandparents' recipe and my suegra's (mother-in-law). My grandparents always made their picadillo with ground beef, whereas my suegra preferred shredded beef.

3 dried ancho or pasilla chiles, stemmed and seeded

2 dried guajillo chiles, stemmed and seeded

3 cups water

Coarse salt

1 tablespoon vegetable oil

2 serrano chiles, seeded and finely chopped (optional)

½ medium white onion, diced

2 garlic cloves, minced

1 pound lean ground beef

3 roma tomatoes, diced

3 medium potatoes, peeled and diced

2 medium carrots, peeled and thinly sliced

1 cup cooked nopales (see step 1 of *Ensalada de Nopales*, page 102, for technique)

1 cup corn kernels

1 cup beef or chicken broth

Warm tortillas, for serving

1 In a medium saucepan, bring the dried chiles and water to a boil over medium-high heat. Cover, reduce the heat to low, and simmer for about 5 minutes, until the chiles have softened. Remove from the heat and cool slightly.

2 Blend the chiles and their cooking water in a blender until smooth. Season with salt.

3 In a Dutch oven or large saucepan, heat the oil over medium-high heat. Add the serrano chiles (if using) and the onion and sauté for 2 to 3 minutes, until translucent. Add the garlic and sauté for an additional 30 seconds. Stir in the ground beef, breaking it up into pieces with the back of a wooden spoon, and cook for about 5 minutes, until it is no longer pink. Stir in the tomatoes, potatoes, carrots, nopales, corn, chile purée, and beef broth. Season with ½ to 1 teaspoon of salt. Bring the picadillo to a boil and adjust the seasoning, if necessary. Cover, reduce the heat to low, and simmer for 20 to 25 minutes, or until the carrots and potatoes are fork-tender.

4 Ladle into bowls and serve with warm tortillas.

TIP *For my suegra's shredded beef picadillo, substitute 2 to 3 cups shredded beef (finely chopped) and omit the vegetables. Garnish with chopped white onion and cilantro.*

BEEF, PORK & MORE

LAMB BIRRIA ESTILO YAHUALICA

YIELD: 8 SERVINGS PREP TIME: 15 MINUTES COOK TIME: 6 TO 8 HOURS

Birria is a slow-roasted goat or lamb delicacy. Most birria recipes include a dried chile adobo, but in Yahualica (the small town I call home), the lamb is roasted with very few spices to enhance the intense smoky flavor of the meat. The meat is shredded into bite-size pieces and topped with chopped white onion, crushed oregano, and a mild tomato salsa.

Cooking spray
2½ to 3 pounds lamb shoulder roast
Salt
Freshly ground black pepper
2 tablespoons vegetable oil
2 cups beef broth or water
1 teaspoon crushed Mexican oregano, plus more for garnish
1 large white onion, thinly sliced
3 garlic cloves, minced
2 bay leaves
Handful cilantro leaves
Salsa de Tomate (page 142)
Chopped white onion, for garnish
Warm tortillas for serving
Chiles Torreados (page 135)

1 Lightly grease inside of slow cooker with cooking spray.

2 Season the lamb shoulder generously with salt and pepper.

3 In a large nonstick skillet, heat the oil over high heat. Add the lamb and sear, 4 to 5 minutes, until browned on all sides.

4 Transfer the lamb to the slow cooker. Pour the beef broth over and sprinkle the oregano evenly over the lamb. Top with the onion, garlic, bay leaves, and cilantro leaves. Cover and cook on the high-heat setting for 6 to 8 hours, until the meat shreds easily. Shred the meat into bite-size pieces.

5 Spoon some shredded lamb into a bowl. Ladle about ¼ cup of the broth and ⅓ cup *Salsa de Tomate* over. Garnish with chopped white onion and oregano. Serve with warm corn tortillas and *Chiles Torreados*.

TIP Substitute goat for an equally intensely flavored birria. But if you prefer a milder flavor, pork (shoulder or Boston butt roast) or beef (tri-tip roast or boneless country-style ribs) can also be substituted. Birria de Pollo (made with boneless, skinless chicken breasts) is often served as an option for those who don't eat red meat.

MILANESAS DE RES

YIELD: 4 TO 6 SERVINGS   PREP TIME: 15 MINUTES   COOK TIME: 20 MINUTES

A simple, tasty, and versatile dish, milanesas *are thin-cut slices of steak coated in bread crumbs and fried to an enticing golden brown. Serve with your choice of sides, like* Calabacitas *(page 111), or* Black Bean Salad with Corn and Nopales *(page 103), and a spicy salsa, as a filling for sandwiches (*tortas de milanesa*), or serve it thinly sliced as a filling for tacos. Milanesas can also be made with pork or chicken, and I like to switch up the coatings (see the tip).*

2 large eggs
¼ cup milk
1 garlic clove, minced
Salt
½ teaspoon freshly ground
  black pepper, plus more
  for seasoning
1½ cups dried bread crumbs
  or panko
1 tablespoon ancho
  chile powder
1 teaspoon seasoning salt
1 to 1½ pounds thin-cut
  round steak
3 to 4 tablespoons
  vegetable oil, for frying

1 In a wide bowl, whisk together the eggs and milk. Stir in the garlic and season with salt and pepper. Set aside.

2 In a shallow baking dish or pie plate, mix together the bread crumbs, ancho chile powder, seasoning salt, and ½ teaspoon pepper.

3 Dip the steaks, one at a time, in the egg mixture, then into the seasoned bread crumbs, coating both sides. Transfer the steaks to large plate.

4 In a large nonstick skillet, heat at least 2 tablespoons of the oil over medium-high heat. Fry the steaks, in batches if necessary, for 5 to 7 minutes per side, until golden brown. Transfer to a paper towel–lined plate to drain excess oil. Repeat with the remaining milanesas, adding more vegetable oil to the pan if needed.

5 Serve with your choice of sides and your favorite salsa.

TIP If making pork milanesas, substitute masa harina for the bread crumbs; for chicken milanesas, use cornflake crumbs.

PORK CHORIZO

YIELD: 4 TO 6 SERVINGS   PREP TIME: 5 MINUTES   COOK TIME: 15 MINUTES

Aside from her famous flour tortillas and shredded beef tamales with black olives tucked inside, Gramm (my grandmother) was also known for her homemade pork chorizo. The heady aroma of vinegar, chiles, and spices takes me back to Gramm's cozy kitchen every time I make chorizo from scratch.

2 dried ancho chiles, stemmed and seeded

2 dried guajillo chiles, stemmed and seeded

2 dried chiles de árbol, stemmed (optional)

2 cups water

⅓ cup white vinegar

1 pound ground pork (20% fat)

2 garlic cloves, minced

1 teaspoon ground cumin

1 teaspoon ground oregano

1 teaspoon salt

½ teaspoon freshly ground black pepper

¼ teaspoon ground cloves

1 to 2 tablespoons vegetable oil

Scrambled eggs, for serving

Refried Beans (page 96), for serving

Cooked nopales (see step 1 of Ensalada de Nopales, page 102, for technique), for serving

1 In a medium saucepan, bring the dried chiles and water to a boil over high heat. Cover, reduce the heat to low, and simmer for about 5 minutes, until the chiles have softened. Remove from the heat and let cool slightly.

2 Remove the chiles with a slotted spoon and transfer to a blender or food processor. Blend the chiles with the vinegar until smooth.

3 In a large bowl, mix together the ground pork, chile purée, garlic, cumin, oregano, salt, pepper, and cloves.

4 Cover with plastic wrap and refrigerate for at least 3 hours, allowing the flavors to develop.

5 In a nonstick skillet, heat the oil over medium-high heat. Add the chorizo and cook, breaking it up with the back of a wooden spoon, for about 5 minutes, until browned.

6 Serve with scrambled eggs, *Refried Beans*, cooked nopales, or as a filling for tacos.

TIP Substitute the ground pork with finely chopped boneless pork to make Mexican longaniza. Also, you can freeze the uncooked chorizo and use in other recipes, like Queso Fundido (page 57) and Tinga de Cerdo (page 58).

QUESO FUNDIDO

YIELD: 4 TO 6 SERVINGS   PREP TIME: 10 MINUTES   COOK TIME: 30 MINUTES

Queso Fundido is the ultimate in cheesy goodness. Crumbled Mexican chorizo topped with lots of melted cheese is traditionally served as an appetizer with totopos *(tortilla chips) or as a main dish served with warm tortillas. I like to go all out with my queso fundido, adding onion, mushrooms, roasted green chiles, and a splash of tequila. Sometimes referred to as Mexican fondue, queso fundido is ideal for enjoying with friends. Although, it's so good, you might not want to share.*

2 Anaheim chiles

1 tablespoon vegetable oil

6 ounces Mexican *Pork Chorizo* (page 56)

1 cup sliced mushrooms

¼ medium red onion, finely chopped

1 garlic clove, minced

2 ounces tequila *añejo* or *reposado*

Salt

1½ cups shredded queso Chihuahua or mild cheddar

1½ cups shredded queso Oaxaca or mozzarella

1 Heat a comal, griddle, or nonstick skillet over high heat. Add the Anaheim chiles and roast, turning occasionally, until completely charred. Transfer the chiles to a plastic or paper bag and let sit for 5 minutes. Using your fingers, or a paper towel, peel off the charred skins. Remove the stems and seeds and cut the chiles into thin slices.

2 Preheat the oven to 375°F.

3 In a medium heat-proof skillet, heat the oil over medium-high heat. Add the chorizo and cook for about 5 minutes, until it is lightly browned. Stir in the roasted chiles, mushrooms, onion, and garlic, and cook, stirring occasionally, for 2 to 3 minutes, until the onion starts to turn translucent. Stir in the tequila and season with salt. Cover, reduce the heat to low, and simmer for 5 minutes.

4 Sprinkle the cheeses over the chorizo. Bake uncovered for 10 to 12 minutes, until the cheese starts to bubble.

TIP *Transform this into a meatless meal by using soy chorizo.*

TINGA DE CERDO

YIELD: 4 TO 6 SERVINGS   PREP TIME: 15 MINUTES   COOK TIME: 30 MINUTES

Tinga de Cerdo *is a great way to use up leftover pork roast or carnitas. Simmered in a tangy chipotle sauce with Mexican pork chorizo, this quick and easy dish tastes like you spent hours in the kitchen. This recipe calls for making the sauce from scratch, but you can save even more time by using canned mild salsa verde and puréeing it with the chipotles. If canned chipotles are too spicy for your taste, simply add a couple of tablespoons of the adobo sauce.*

1 pound tomatillos, husks removed

3 cups water

2 canned chipotles in adobo sauce

1 tablespoon vegetable oil

8 ounces Mexican *Pork Chorizo* (page 56), casing removed if using store-bought

½ medium onion, thinly sliced

1 garlic clove, minced

3 cups shredded pork (leftover carnitas or pork roast)

Salt

Espinacas con Queso (page 119)

Refried Beans (page 96)

1 In a medium saucepan, bring the tomatillos and water to a simmer over medium-high heat. Simmer until cooked through. Remove from the heat and cool slightly.

2 Blend the tomatillos and their cooking water and the chipotles in a blender until smooth.

3 In a large nonstick skillet, heat the oil over medium heat. Add the chorizo and cook, using the back of a wooden spoon to break it up, for 8 to 10 minutes, until fully cooked. Add the onion and cook, stirring occasionally, for 3 to 5 minutes until the onion starts to turn translucent. Add the garlic and cook for an additional 30 seconds. Add the pork and tomatillo-chipotle sauce and season with salt. Cover and simmer for 12 to 15 minutes.

4 Serve with *Espinacas con Queso* and *Refried Beans*.

TIP   *If serving as a filling for tacos, tostadas, or tortas, garnish with chopped red onion, cilantro, shredded lettuce, crumbled queso fresco, Guacamole de Molcajete (page 137), and Mexican crema.*

GOAT VS BEEF

Goat (called either cabrito or chivo in Spanish) is a popular option at many taquerías, especially in the states of Nuevo León, Chihuahua, and Sonora in the northern region of Mexico. Cabrito asado (roast goat) and birria de chivo (goat birria) are two of the most popular dishes featuring goat.

Cabrito asado is made by slow roasting a young goat (kid) on a spit over a low wood-burning flame. The goat is then cut into large pieces and served with lime wedges, grilled chiles and onions, and warm flour tortillas.

For birria, the goat is seasoned with an adobo made from a variety of dried chiles and spices, then covered with hojas de maguey (leaves of the maguey plant) and slow roasted in an underground pit. Once fully cooked, the meat is cut into bite-size pieces and served with a spicy ancho chile salsa and warm corn tortillas.

If you've never tried goat, the texture is similar to beef, while the flavor is much richer, although it can be a little gamey depending on the age of the goat. The older the goat, the stronger the flavor. The first time I tried goat at a roadside stand selling cabrito asado, I didn't like it at all. I don't know if it was because it was when I was still a picky eater, if maybe we had gotten an older goat, or if the gamey flavor truly was that overwhelming. Nevertheless, it took me a couple of years to work up the nerve to try it again. And I am so glad I finally did. Nowadays, I love roast goat! It's meaty, tender, and juicy. You know that incredible flavor when you bite into a piece of an exceptionally delicious grilled steak that's so good even the fat melts in your mouth? That is what goat tastes like, only way better.

If you're looking to branch out and try something new, goat is one tasty option I hope you'll try.

FOUR
CHICKEN & FISH

▽ ▽ ▽ ▽ ▽ ▽ ▽ ▽ ▽ ▽ ▽ ▽ ▽ ▽ ▽ ▽ ▽ ▽ ▽ ▽ ▽ ▽ ▽ ▽ ▽ ▽

This chapter has a little something for anyone who loves chicken and fish, from Beer Batter–Fried Tilapia (page 64) and Atún al Chipotle (page 63) to baked Pollo Adobado con Papas (page 86) and Oven-Roasted Camarones al Mojo de Ajo (page 81). Like the previous chapter, all the dishes included in this chapter are delicious served as main dishes with your favorite sides, but they can also be served as fillings for tacos.

Make classic Mexican dishes like Caldo de Pollo (page 68), spicy Camarones a la Diabla (page 69), and Mole Dulce (page 78).

Add recipes like Brochetas de Pollo con Mango (page 66), Pescado Zarandeado (page 82), and Pollo Asado (page 85) to the menu for your next barbeque.

If you're looking for new ways to serve chicken, try Chicken Pipián Verde (page 72) and Rojo (page 74), Tinga de Pollo (page 90), and Salpicón (page 89). These recipes are also a great way to use up leftover rotisserie chicken and Thanksgiving turkey.

¡Buen provecho!

CHICKEN & FISH

ATÚN AL CHIPOTLE

YIELD: 4 SERVINGS   PREP TIME: 5 MINUTES   COOK TIME: 20 MINUTES

This saucy chipotle tuna dish is a super quick and easy dinner option for those days when you need to get dinner on the table in a hurry and takeout just isn't an option. On busy days like those, I'm glad I always have canned tuna in my pantry. With a few staple ingredients from your refrigerator and pantry—like tomatoes, onions, and canned chipotle peppers—you can have a delicious meal on the table in about 20 minutes.

1 cup mild *Salsa de Tomate* (page 142) or 1 (8-ounce) can tomato sauce

2 canned chipotle peppers in adobo

1 tablespoon vegetable oil

½ medium onion, finely chopped

1 to 2 serrano chiles, seeded and coarsely chopped

3 (5-ounce) cans water-packed tuna, drained

3 roma tomatoes, coarsely chopped

Salt

Freshly ground black pepper

12 pimiento-stuffed olives, sliced

Refried Beans (page 96)

Guacamole de Molcajete (page 137)

1 Blend the salsa and chipotle peppers in a blender until smooth. (If using tomato sauce, add 1 can of water to the purée mixture.)

2 In a medium nonstick skillet, heat the oil over medium-high heat. Add the onion and serrano chiles and sauté for 2 to 3 minutes, until the onion turns translucent. Add the tuna, tomatoes, and the chipotle purée, and season with salt and pepper. Cover, reduce the heat to low, simmer for 12 to 15 minutes, until sauce reduces slightly. Stir in the olives.

3 Serve with *Refried Beans* and *Guacamole de Molcajete*. If serving as a filling for tacos, garnish with chopped red onion, cilantro, and *Salsa Cruda* (page 140).

TIP *Stir this saucy chipotle tuna into cooked pasta for another quick and easy dinner option.*

BEER BATTER-FRIED TILAPIA

YIELD: 6 SERVINGS   PREP TIME: 10 MINUTES   COOK TIME: 20 MINUTES

Batter-fried fish tacos are popular in many of the coastal states of Mexico, especially in towns that cater to tourists like Ensenada and La Paz, hence the name Baja-style fish tacos. If you've never heard of or tried a Baja-style fish taco, they are made with tender pieces of fish dipped in a light and tangy batter made with Mexican beer. The tacos are served on either flour or corn tortillas and garnished with fresh pico de gallo, shredded cabbage, and slices of ripe avocado.

The secret is in the batter. The fish should be crisp and golden on the outside, while tender and moist on the inside. The yeast in the beer is what makes the batter so light and airy, while the baking soda helps crisp things up. Some people prefer to add egg to their batter, but I feel that it causes the batter to get soft as it cools.

The best thing about this batter is that it's not just for fish. You can dip pretty much anything in this batter for a tasty treat. Shrimp, bite-size pieces of cooked chicken, and fresh veggies like cauliflower and zucchini are just a few of my favorite things to fry in this beer batter.

1½ cups all-purpose flour, divided
1½ teaspoons salt, divided
2 teaspoons ancho chile powder
1 teaspoon baking powder
1 teaspoon crushed Mexican oregano

½ teaspoon ground cumin
1 (12-ounce) bottle dark Mexican beer
1 tablespoon mustard
2 cups vegetable oil, for frying
6 tilapia fillets, thawed if frozen

Lime wedges
Pico de Gallo (page 139)
Shredded cabbage
Warmed corn or flour tortillas
Arroz Mexicano (page 100)

1 In a wide bowl, combine ½ cup of flour and ½ teaspoon of salt. Set aside.

2 In a large bowl, mix together the remaining 1 cup of the flour, chile powder, remaining 1 teaspoon of the salt, baking powder, oregano, and ground cumin. Slowly whisk in the beer and mustard.

3 In a large nonstick skillet, heat the oil over medium-high heat.

4 Coat each tilapia fillet in the flour mixture, making sure both sides are evenly coated, then dip the fillets into the beer batter.

5 Fry the fillets, two or three at a time, in the hot oil for 3 to 5 minutes per side, until golden brown on both sides. Transfer the fried fillets to a paper towel–lined plate to drain any excess oil. Repeat with the remaining fillets.

6 Garnish with lime wedges, *Pico de Gallo*, and shredded cabbage. Serve with warm corn or flour tortillas, *Arroz Mexicano*, and your favorite agua fresca.

TIP *Make* hamburguesas de pescado *by serving the fried fillets on toasted hamburger buns. Garnish with lettuce, tomato, onion, and tartar sauce or* Crema de Chipotle *(page 136).*

BROCHETAS DE POLLO CON MANGO

YIELD: 6 SERVINGS   PREP TIME: 3 HOURS 10 MINUTES   COOK TIME: 15 MINUTES

Every year for Easter we go on a week-long camping trip to el rancho with all of my husband's siblings and their families. Each family is assigned one day of the week to prepare all of the meals for that day. On the last day, we gather all of the leftover meats, veggies, and fruits to make grilled brochetas. *These chicken and mango skewers are one of my favorite flavor combinations made during one of our camping trips.*

2 to 3 canned chipotle peppers
½ cup freshly squeezed orange juice
¼ cup freshly squeezed lime juice
¼ cup tequila
2 tablespoons maple syrup
2 tablespoons vegetable oil

2 garlic cloves, minced
1 teaspoon salt
½ teaspoon freshly ground black pepper
1½ pounds boneless, skinless chicken breasts, cut into 2-inch pieces
3 large mangos, peeled, seeded, and cut into 2-inch chunks

2 green bell peppers, cut into 2-inch chunks
1 large onion, cut into 2-inch chunks
1 red bell pepper, cut into 2-inch chunks
Arroz Mexicano (page 100)

1 Blend the chipotle peppers and orange and lime juices in a blender until smooth. Transfer to a medium bowl. Whisk in the tequila, maple syrup, oil, garlic, salt, and pepper. Reserve ⅓ cup of the marinade.

2 In a 9x13-inch baking dish, arrange the chicken breast pieces and pour the marinade over, tossing to coat. Cover with plastic wrap and refrigerate for at least 3 hours.

3 About 1 hour before grilling time, preheat the grill and soak 12 to 16 bamboo skewers in water.

4 Thread the chicken pieces alternating with chunks of mango, green bell pepper, onion, and red bell pepper until almost full.

5 Grill the brochetas over a medium flame for 3 to 4 minutes per side (about 15 minutes total), brushing occasionally with the reserved marinade, until the chicken is cooked through. Serve 2 to 3 skewers atop *Arroz Mexicano.*

TIP *Remove skewers and serve grilled chicken, mango, and veggies in warm flour tortillas. Garnish with fresh cilantro, Mexican crema, and/or* Guacamole de Molcajete.

CALDO DE POLLO

YIELD: 6 TO 8 SERVINGS   PREP TIME: 15 MINUTES   COOK TIME: 2 HOURS

If you're wondering what a soup recipe is doing in a taco cookbook, here's why: Aside from being a comforting soup that reminds me of the caldos *my grandparents prepared when I was growing up, it's also a great way to add flavor to chicken to use in other dishes included in this chapter. Whenever I make caldo de pollo, I always add a little more chicken just so I can have leftovers to use in other recipes.*

2 to 2½ pounds bone-in, skin-on chicken breast, whole or cut up

12 cups water

2 ears corn, cut into 3 or 4 pieces

½ medium onion, chopped

2 garlic cloves, lightly mashed

Handful cilantro sprigs

2 teaspoons salt

½ teaspoon black pepper

3 medium carrots, peeled and cut into ½-inch chunks

3 medium potatoes, peeled and cut into ½-inch chunks

3 medium Mexican calabacitas, cut into 1-inch slices

Lime wedges, for garnish

Cooked nopales, for garnish (see step 1 of *Ensalada de Nopales*, page 102, for technique)

Warm corn tortillas

1 In a large soup pot, add the chicken, 8 cups water, corn, onion, garlic, and cilantro, and season with salt and pepper. Bring to a boil over high heat, skimming off and discarding any foam that rises to the top. Cover, reduce the heat to low, and simmer for 60 to 90 minutes until the chicken is fully cooked and tender. (If using chicken to shred in another recipe, remove from the heat, let cool, and shred.)

2 Remove the chicken from pot. Discard the onion, garlic, and cilantro. Add the carrots, potatoes, and calabacitas; cover; and simmer while you shred the chicken into bite-size pieces, discarding the skin and bones.

3 Return the shredded chicken to the pot. Add 2 to 4 cups of the water, depending on how much broth you prefer, if necessary. Adjust the seasoning, if needed, and simmer for 15 to 20 minutes.

4 Ladle the soup into bowls. Garnish with lime wedges and cooked nopales. Serve with warm corn tortillas.

TIP *Strain and the cooled broth into 2-cup containers and refrigerate for up to a week to add to recipes calling for chicken broth.*

CAMARONES A LA DIABLA

YIELD: 6 TO 8 SERVINGS   PREP TIME: 10 MINUTES   COOK TIME: 40 MINUTES

Camarones a la Diabla *are hot as the devil with a fiery sauce made with tomatoes, chile guajillo, and lots of spicy chile de árbol. This traditional shrimp dish is a popular menu option at many Mexican seafood restaurants, where you are always asked how spicy you want it. For those who are weary of spicy foods, only 1 or 2 árbol chiles are added to the sauce for flavor, but for those who want a sauce as scorching hot as the sun, add as many chiles as you can handle.*

6 roma tomatoes

2 dried guajillo chiles, stemmed and seeded

2 to 12 dried chiles de árbol, stemmed

3 cups water

1 tablespoon butter

1 tablespoon olive oil

½ medium onion, thinly sliced

2 garlic cloves, minced

2 pounds shrimp, deveined

Salt

Arroz Mexicano (page 100)

Ensalada de Nopales (page 102)

Crusty garlic bread or tostadas

1 In a medium saucepan, bring the tomatoes, guajillo chiles, chiles de árbol, and water to a boil, reduce the heat to low, and simmer 10 to 12 minutes, until the tomatoes are fully cooked. Remove from the heat and cool slightly. Blend the tomatoes, chiles, and their cooking water in a blender until smooth.

2 In a large skillet, heat the butter and olive oil over high heat. Add the onion and sauté for 2 to 3 minutes, stirring occasionally, until the onion turns translucent. Add the garlic and shrimp, and sauté until the shrimp turns pink. Reduce the heat to low, pour in the chile sauce, and season with salt. Cover and simmer 8 to 10 minutes, until the sauce reduces slightly.

3 Serve with *Arroz Mexicano, Ensalada de Nopales,* and crusty garlic bread or tostadas.

TIP *This dish is already known for being super spicy, but in case you want to up the heat even more, finely chop a fresh habanero pepper and add it in with the onion.*

CAMARONES A LA MEXICANA

YIELD: 4 SERVINGS   PREP TIME: 5 MINUTES   COOK TIME: 25 MINUTES

Camarones a la Mexicana *is a traditional Mexican dish that gets its name "a la Mexicana" because the red, white, and green of the vegetables are representative of the colors of the Mexican flag. A popular dish at seafood restaurants all throughout Mexico, camarones a la mexicana is a bright and colorful guisado that can be served on its own with* Arroz Mexicano *and nopales on the side or as a filling for tacos.*

2 tablespoons olive oil
½ medium onion, chopped
1 green bell pepper, chopped
2 serrano chiles, finely chopped (optional)
1 garlic clove, chopped
1 pound medium shrimp, peeled and deveined
3 roma tomatoes, chopped
1 cup tomato-based salsa
4 cilantro sprigs
Salt

In a large skillet, heat the olive oil over high heat. Add the onion, bell pepper, and serrano chiles (if using), and sauté for 3 to 5 minutes, until slightly tender. Add the garlic and shrimp and cook, stirring occasionally, about 2 minutes, until the shrimp turn pink. Stir in the tomatoes, salsa, and cilantro, and season lightly with salt. Once the mixture starts to boil, reduce the heat to low, cover the skillet, and simmer for 10 to 15 minutes, until the sauce has thickened slightly.

TIP *Increase tomato salsa to 2 cups and stir in 1 cup of cooked white rice for a flavorful shrimp stew.*

CAMARONES ENCHILADOS

YIELD: 6 TO 8 SERVINGS   PREP TIME: 5 MINUTES   COOK TIME: 15 MINUTES

These spicy baked shrimp are a cinch to whip up, and they cook up pretty quickly, too. My favorite bottled hot sauces to use in this recipe are Valentina and Tapatío brands, but you can use your favorite bottled salsa or wing sauce. These shrimp are so good you won't be able to resist snacking on them. Thread two or three camarones enchilados onto a bamboo skewer to garnish an icy cold Michelada *(page 190).*

Cooking spray
4 tablespoons unsalted
   butter, melted
½ cup bottled hot
   sauce (Valentina or
   Tapatío brands)
2 tablespoons cilantro,
   finely chopped
1 garlic clove, minced
Salt
2 pounds shrimp, deveined
Freshly ground black pepper
Lime wedges, for garnish
Warmed tortillas,
   for serving
Frijoles Borrachos (page 101)
Ensalada de Nopales
   (page 102)

1 Preheat the oven to 400°F. Lightly grease a baking sheet with cooking spray.

2 In a medium bowl, whisk together the melted butter, hot sauce, cilantro, and garlic. Season with salt.

3 In a large bowl, season the shrimp with salt and pepper. Pour the sauce over the shrimp, stirring to coat.

4 Spread the shrimp out in a single layer on the prepared baking sheet. Bake for 12 to 15 minutes, until cooked through and lightly browned.

5 Garnish with lime wedges and serve with warm tortillas, *Frijoles Borrachos,* and *Ensalada de Nopales.*

TIP *Thread the shrimp on skewers and grill over a medium flame for 3 to 5 minutes per side, until completely cooked and lightly browned.*

CHICKEN & FISH

CHICKEN PIPIÁN VERDE

YIELD: 6 SERVINGS   PREP TIME: 30 MINUTES   COOK TIME: 25 MINUTES

Pipián Verde is an exquisite traditional Mexican sauce made with roasted poblano peppers, tomatillos, and pepitas and served over chicken, turkey, or fish. The pepitas give pipián its distinctive texture. I make my sauce completely from scratch, but if you're pressed for time you could always use canned green enchilada sauce. Chicken pipián verde is the perfect recipe for those nights when you're looking for something out of the ordinary to wow your friends and family.

3 poblano peppers
12 to 15 tomatillos
2 serrano chiles, stemmed
4 cups water
½ medium onion, chopped
1 garlic clove, minced
Handful cilantro leaves
¾ cup pepitas (hulled
   pumpkin seeds)
4 tablespoons masa harina
4 cups chicken broth,
   divided
Salt
Freshly ground black pepper
2 tablespoons vegetable oil
4 boneless, skinless chicken
   breasts, cooked and cut
   into bite-size pieces
Arroz Mexicano (page 100)
Warmed tortillas,
   for serving

1 On a comal or nonstick skillet, roast the poblano peppers over medium-high heat until blistered and charred all over. Put the peppers in a zip-top bag and let sit for 5 minutes. Using your fingers or paper towels, peel the charred skin from the peppers. Remove the stems and seeds.

2 In a medium saucepan, bring the tomatillos, serrano chiles, and water to a boil over medium-high heat. Cover, reduce the heat to low, and simmer for about 15 minutes, until the tomatillos are completely cooked. Remove from the heat and cool slightly.

3 Transfer the tomatillos and serrano chiles with a slotted spoon to a blender. Add the peeled roasted poblano peppers, onion, garlic, cilantro, pepitas, masa harina, and 2 cups of the chicken broth, and blend until smooth.

4 In a large, deep skillet or saucepan, heat the oil over medium heat. Add the tomato-chile sauce. Season with salt and pepper and stir to combine. The sauce should be the consistency of heavy cream. If it's too thick, add more chicken broth until it reaches the desired consistency. Continue to cook, stirring occasionally, until the sauce begins to boil. Add the chicken and reduce the heat to low. Cover and simmer for 15 to 20 minutes, until the chicken is heated through.

5 Serve with warm tortillas and *Arroz Mexicano*.

TIP *Substitute 3 to 4 cups shredded leftover Thanksgiving turkey for the chicken.*

CHICKEN PIPIÁN ROJO

YIELD: 6 SERVINGS   PREP TIME: 15 MINUTES   COOK TIME: 30 MINUTES

Pipián is a traditional Mexican sauce that gets its distinct grainy texture from the pepitas (pumpkin seeds). Pipián Rojo is made with tomatoes and dried ancho chiles. Traditionally pipián is served over fish, shrimp, roasted pork, or chicken. But it can also be used as a filling for tacos, burritos, sopes, and empanadas. Serve pipián rojo with white rice or cooked pasta and Espinacas con Queso (page 119), or, when using as a filling for tacos, garnished with chopped red onion and cilantro.

3 roma tomatoes, cut into quarters

3 dried ancho chiles, stemmed and seeded

3 cups water

5 cups chicken broth, divided

½ medium onion, chopped

2 garlic cloves

¾ cup pepitas (hulled pumpkin seeds)

¼ cup masa harina

2 tablespoons vegetable oil

Salt

½ teaspoon freshly ground black pepper

¼ teaspoon ground cumin

⅛ teaspoon ground cloves

3 to 4 cups shredded cooked chicken

Warmed corn tortillas, for serving

1 In a medium saucepan, bring the tomatoes, dried ancho chiles, and water to a boil over medium-high heat. Cook for 12 to 15 minutes, until the tomatoes are cooked through and the chiles have softened. Remove from the heat and cool slightly.

2 Blend the cooked tomatoes, chiles, their cooking water, 2 cups of chicken broth, the onion, garlic, pepitas, and masa harina in a blender until smooth.

3 In a large, deep skillet, heat the oil over medium-high heat. Add the tomato-chile purée and stir with a wire whisk or wooden spoon to combine. Stir in 2 to 3 more cups of the remaining chicken broth until the pipián sauce reaches the desired consistency.

4 Season with salt, pepper, cumin, and cloves, and then reduce the heat to low. Add the cooked chicken, cover, and simmer, stirring occasionally to prevent the sauce from sticking, for about 15 minutes, until heated through.

5 Serve with warm corn tortillas.

TIP For a different taste, substitute 3 to 4 cups of shredded beef or pork for the chicken.

TAQUERÍA TACOS

LANGOSTA AL TEQUILA

YIELD: 4 SERVINGS   PREP TIME: 5 MINUTES   COOK TIME: 15 MINUTES

The first time my husband and I splurged on lobster tails at the grocery store for our first wedding anniversary, we had no idea how to cook them. I had eaten tacos de langosta a couple of times as a kid during trips with my grandparents to Ensenada and San Felipe, but I never cooked the lobster myself. Through a lot of trial and error, we finally ended up with a very simple recipe for great-tasting lobster tails that we both loved.

4 lobster tails, fresh
  or thawed, halved
  lengthwise
Salt
Freshly ground black pepper
4 tablespoons butter
1 garlic clove, minced
2 ounces tequila
2 ounces lime juice
1 teaspoon dried parsley
Arroz Mexicano (page 100)
Lime wedges, for serving
Fresh salad, for serving

1 Season the inside of the lobster tails with salt and pepper.

2 In a large nonstick skillet, melt the butter over medium-high heat. Add the garlic and sauté for 30 seconds. Stir in the tequila, lime juice, and parsley. Arrange the lobster tails meat-side down in the skillet and cook for 3 to 5 minutes. Turn the tails over and continue to cook for another 3 to 5 minutes, until cooked through.

3 Serve atop *Arroz Mexicano* with lime wedges and a fresh salad.

TIP *Serve bite-size pieces of lobster in a warm soft taco–size flour tortilla. Top with shredded asadero cheese, sliced avocado, shredded cabbage, and* Crema de Chipotle *(page 136).*

MOLE RANCHERO

YIELD: 6 TO 8 SERVINGS   PREP TIME: 30 MINUTES   COOK TIME: 30 MINUTES

All moles are not created equal. Some traditional mole recipes include up to 40 ingredients. This Mole Ranchero *is one of the easiest mole recipes to make as it is made with just a handful of ingredients. Unlike* Mole Dulce *(page 78), mole ranchero isn't sweet and does not contain chocolate. And while mole dulce is usually served with chicken or turkey, mole ranchero can be served with chicken, pork, beef, and even seafood. To serve in tacos, garnish with chopped red onion and cilantro.*

6 cups chicken broth

4 or 5 tablespoons vegetable oil, divided

3 dried ancho chiles, stemmed and seeded

2 dried guajillo chiles, stemmed and seeded

4 roma tomatoes

4 tomatillos

½ medium white onion, cut into quarters

2 garlic cloves

3 corn tortillas, cut into wedges

1 teaspoon salt

½ teaspoon black pepper

½ teaspoon ground cumin

¼ teaspoon crushed Mexican oregano

2 pounds cooked chicken pieces or 4 cups shredded chicken

Arroz Mexicano (page 100), for serving

Refried Beans (page 96), for serving

Warmed tortillas, for serving

1 In a medium saucepan, simmer the chicken broth over medium-high heat until heated through.

2 In large nonstick skillet, heat 2 tablespoons of the oil over medium-high heat. Add the dried chiles and sauté for about 30 seconds per side. Transfer the chiles to a large heat-proof bowl. Add the tomatoes and tomatillos to the skillet, adding 1 tablespoon of the remaining oil, if necessary, and cook for 5 to 7 minutes, until lightly charred.

3 Add the onion and garlic and sauté for 2 to 3 minutes until the onion is translucent. Transfer to the bowl with the chiles.

4 Add 1 tablespoon of the remaining oil and fry the tortilla pieces until golden and slightly crisp. Transfer to the bowl.

5 Pour 3 cups of the hot chicken broth over ingredients in the bowl and let sit for 10 to 15 minutes, until the chiles have softened completely. Blend the soaked ingredients in a blender until smooth.

6 In a Dutch oven or large saucepan, heat the remaining 1 to 2 tablespoons of the oil. Strain the mole sauce into the Dutch oven, stirring constantly to prevent the mole from sticking or clumping. Stir in the remaining 3 cups of chicken broth, salt, pepper, cumin, and oregano. Simmer the mole sauce, stirring occasionally, for 8 to 10 minutes, until it thickens and starts to boil.

7 Add the cooked chicken pieces to the sauce and adjust the seasoning, if necessary. Cover, reduce the heat to low, and simmer for 15 to 20 minutes.

8 Serve with *Arroz Mexicano*, *Refried Beans*, and warm tortillas.

TIP *Substitute 4 cups leftover pork carnitas (cut into bite-size pieces) for the chicken, and stir in 1 cup baby spinach leaves just before serving.*

MOLE DULCE

During my suegra's first trip to the Unites States, I asked her to share some of her favorite authentic Mexican recipes so I could make them for my husband. One recipe I really wanted to learn to make was mole, because it was a dish neither of my grandparents ever made from scratch. I add 2 pounds of cooked chicken to my mole, but this recipe is also great to use with rotisserie chicken or leftover Thanksgiving turkey.

6 cups chicken broth

6 tablespoons vegetable oil, divided

4 dried ancho chiles, stemmed and seeded

3 roma tomatoes, cut into quarters

6 tomatillos, husks removed

2 garlic cloves

¼ cup unsalted peanuts or pepitas

1 day-old bolillo roll, cut into 1-inch slices

1 (3-inch) cinnamon stick

1 (3 pound) tablet Mexican chocolate, cut into 8 wedges

1 teaspoon salt

½ teaspoon freshly ground black pepper

½ teaspoon ground cinnamon

¼ teaspoon ground cloves

¼ cup granulated sugar

2 pounds cooked chicken pieces or 4 cups shredded chicken

2 tablespoons sesame seeds

Arroz Mexicano (page 100), for serving

Warmed tortillas, for serving

1 In a medium saucepan, simmer the chicken broth over medium-high heat until heated through.

2 In large nonstick skillet, heat 2 tablespoons of the oil over medium-high heat. Add the dried chiles and sauté for about 30 seconds per side. Transfer to a large heat-proof bowl.

3 Add the tomatoes and tomatillos to the skillet, adding 1 tablespoon of the remaining oil, if necessary, and cook for about 5 minutes, until lightly charred. Transfer to the bowl with the chiles.

4 Add the garlic and peanuts cook for about 1 minute. Transfer to bowl with the other ingredients.

5 Add 1 tablespoon of the oil and cook the bolillo until lightly toasted. Remove from the heat and transfer to the bowl.

6 Add the cinnamon stick and Mexican chocolate to the bowl with the heated ingredients. Pour about 3 cups of hot chicken broth over, and let sit for 10 to 15 minutes, until the chiles have softened completely.

7 Blend the soaked ingredients in a blender until smooth.

➤

▽ ▽

8 In a Dutch oven or large saucepan, heat the remaining 2 or 3 tablespoons of the oil over medium-high heat. Strain the mole sauce into the Dutch oven, stirring constantly to prevent the mole from sticking or clumping. Stir in the remaining 3 cups chicken broth, salt, pepper, ground cinnamon, cloves, and sugar. Simmer, stirring occasionally, for 8 to 10 minutes, until the sauce thickens and starts to boil. Add the cooked chicken pieces to the sauce and adjust the seasoning, if necessary. Cover, reduce the heat to low, and simmer for 15 to 20 minutes.

9 In a small nonstick skillet, toast the sesame seeds over low heat for 2 to 3 minutes, until golden brown.

10 Serve the mole with *Arroz Mexicano* and plenty of warm tortillas. Garnish with a sprinkling of toasted sesame seeds.

TIP *For a darker sauce, substitute dried pasilla chiles for the ancho chiles.*

TAQUERÍA TACOS

OVEN-ROASTED CAMARONES AL MOJO DE AJO

YIELD: 6 TO 8 SERVINGS   PREP TIME: 5 MINUTES   COOK TIME: 15 MINUTES

Camarones al Mojo de Ajo *is traditional Mexican shrimp dish in a buttery garlic sauce. This baked version maintains the flavor of the traditional dish, but instead of being simmered on the stove, the shrimp are roasted in the oven. These roasted garlic shrimp can be served atop a crisp green salad for lunch or as a filling for tacos and quesadillas. They are so tasty that I also like to serve them as an appetizer or snack when we have company over.*

Cooking spray
2 pounds shrimp, peeled and deveined
½ cup (1 stick) butter, at room temperature
4 garlic cloves, minced
2 teaspoons dried fine herbs, lightly crushed
Salt
Freshly ground black pepper
Arroz Mexicano (page 100), for serving
Espinacas con Queso (page 119), for serving

1 Preheat the oven to 400°F. Lightly grease a baking sheet with cooking spray.

2 In a large bowl, mix together the shrimp, butter, garlic, and herbs, stirring to coat. Season with salt and pepper.

3 Arrange the shrimp in a single layer on the baking sheet. Bake for 10 to 12 minutes, or until the shrimp are fully cooked. Remove from the oven.

4 Serve with *Arroz Mexicano* and *Espinacas con Queso*.

TIP *Thread the shrimp on skewers alternately with Camarones Enchilados (page 71) as a garnish for Micheladas (page 190).*

PESCADO ZARANDEADO

YIELD: 4 TO 6 SERVINGS   PREP TIME: 10 MINUTES   COOK TIME: 20 MINUTES

This tantalizing grilled delicacy is made with butterflied red snapper. Ask your butcher to clean, scale, and butterfly your fish. We like to grill the fish whole with the head and tail, but if you prefer, ask your butcher to remove them. Traditionally, pescado zarandeado is served on a large platter topped with grilled veggies and plenty of warm tortillas for everyone to make their own tacos. But it's also delicious on its own with a side of fresh green salad.

1 cup ketchup
2 tablespoons mustard
2 tablespoons fresh
   lime juice
1 tablespoon white vinegar
2 garlic cloves, minced
1 teaspoon ancho
   chile powder
1 teaspoon paprika

1 teaspoon salt, divided
1 teaspoon freshly ground
   black pepper, divided
1 (3- to 3½-pound) whole
   red snapper, scaled,
   cleaned, and butterflied
1 large red onion, halved and
   thinly sliced
1 green bell pepper,
   thinly sliced

1 red bell pepper,
   thinly sliced
2 banana peppers, seeded
   and thinly sliced
2 serrano chiles, seeded
   and thinly sliced
Lime wedges, for serving
Warmed tortillas,
   for serving

1 Preheat the grill.

2 In a medium bowl, whisk together the ketchup, mustard, lime juice, vinegar, and garlic. Stir in the ancho chile powder, paprika, ½ teaspoon of the salt, and ½ teaspoon of the pepper.

3 Lay the butterflied fish flat on a large piece of aluminum foil; season lightly with the remaining ½ teaspoon of the salt and the remaining ½ teaspoon of the pepper. Brush the ketchup sauce all over fish, making sure both sides are well coated. Top the fish with the onion, peppers, and chiles. Cover with another large piece of aluminum foil, folding the edges together until the fish is sealed.

4 Place the packet in a grill basket and grill over a medium flame for 15 to 20 minutes, turning the grill basket over every 3 to 5 minutes. Remove from the heat.

5 Carefully open the grill basket and unwrap the fish. Serve with lime wedges and warm tortillas.

TIP *Substitute 1½ cups store-bought Catalina dressing for the home-made sauce.*

PESCADO DORADO

YIELD: 4 TO 6 SERVINGS   PREP TIME: 10 MINUTES   COOK TIME: 20 MINUTES

Another of my favorite dishes to make and enjoy at el rancho is Pescado Dorado *(fried fish). Prepared in a large disco over a wood-burning flame, whole fish are fried to a golden crisp in manteca. Because we need to make enough to feed a crowd, we use about a kilo (two pounds) of manteca and at least a dozen whole fish. Our favorite fish to fry are red snapper, trout, and mojarras (a type of tilapia).*

2 cups manteca or
   vegetable oil, for frying
2 whole red snappers or
   2 to 4 whole trout or
   tilapia, scaled and
   cleaned inside and out
2 to 4 limes, halved
2 to 4 tablespoons
   minced garlic
Salt
Freshly ground black pepper
Lime wedges, for serving
Warmed tortillas,
   for serving
Salsa (your choice),
   for serving
Ensalada de Betabel
   (page 118), for serving

1 In a wok or large nonstick skillet, heat the manteca over medium-high heat.

2 Make three diagonal cuts on each side of the fish. Squeeze the juice of 1 lime over each fish. Rub 1 tablespoon of garlic over each fish; season the fish with salt and pepper.

3 Grab the fish by the tail and carefully submerge in the hot manteca. Fry the fish, 1 or 2 at a time, depending on the size of the pan, for 3 to 5 minutes per side, until golden and crisp. Transfer the fish to a paper towel–lined plate to drain excess oil. Repeat with the remaining fish.

4 Serve with lime wedges, warm tortillas, your favorite salsa, and *Ensalada de Betabel*.

TIP *Frying the fish in manteca adds tons of flavor, but you can also deep-fry them in vegetable oil.*

POLLO ASADO

YIELD: 6 TO 8 SERVINGS   PREP TIME: 3 HOURS 10 MINUTES   COOK TIME: 45 MINUTES

If I were a superhero, grilled chicken would be my kryptonite. My mom worked as a grill master at a restaurant during my teenage years and often stopped by my grandparents' house with a plate of leftovers. Everything mom made on the grill was delicious, but the chicken was my favorite. I never did get the recipe for her marinade, but after a lot of trial and error, I'm pretty darn close. This Pollo Asado recipe can be grilled or baked at 375°F in the oven until fully cooked.

4 dried guajillo chiles,
  stemmed and seeded
2 cups water
1 cup orange juice
1 cup pineapple juice
¼ cup lime juice
2 tablespoons white vinegar
1 (2-pound) whole chicken,
  cut into 8 pieces
1 medium onion,
  thinly sliced
2 garlic cloves, minced
½ cup cilantro,
  finely chopped
1 teaspoon coarse salt
1 teaspoon crushed
  Mexican oregano
1 teaspoon ground cumin
½ teaspoon black pepper

1 In a small saucepan, bring the dried chiles and water to a boil over medium-high heat. Cover, reduce the heat to low, and simmer for 5 minutes until the chiles have softened. Remove from the heat and cool slightly.

2 Blend the chiles, orange juice, pineapple juice, lime juice, and vinegar in a blender until smooth.

3 In a 9x13-inch baking dish, add the chicken pieces, onion, garlic, and cilantro. Pour the chile purée over the chicken, stirring to coat. Season with salt, oregano, cumin, and pepper, and toss to coat. Cover with plastic wrap and refrigerate for at least 3 hours, turning the chicken over after 90 minutes.

4 Preheat the grill.

5 Grill the chicken pieces over a medium flame, turning occasionally, for 30 to 40 minutes, until the chicken is cooked through.

 Darker meats like legs and thighs take more time to cook than chicken breast.

DAIRY FREE

POLLO ADOBADO CON PAPAS

YIELD: 6 TO 8 SERVINGS   PREP TIME: 20 MINUTES   COOK TIME: 1 HOUR

This is a little bit spicy, more than a little saucy, and, if you're like my kids, who love to eat this with their hands, a little bit messy. But it is a whole lot of deliciousness. It's sure to score a touchdown with your family! It bakes great in a conventional oven, and I've even baked it in the big clay oven at the ranch. If you don't feel like turning on the oven, just use your crockpot (6 to 8 hours on low).

3 dried ancho chiles,
stemmed and seeded
2 dried guajillo chiles,
stemmed and seeded
3 cups water
1 cup fresh orange juice
¼ cup fresh lime juice
1 medium onion,
roughly chopped
2 garlic cloves, minced

1 teaspoon crushed
Mexican oregano
1 teaspoon ground cumin
½ teaspoon salt, plus more
for seasoning
½ teaspoon freshly ground
black pepper, plus more
for seasoning
Cooking spray

1 (2-pound) whole chicken,
cut into 8 pieces
6 medium potatoes, cut
into wedges
Warmed tortillas,
for serving
Arroz Mexicano (page 100),
for serving
*Black Bean Salad with Corn
and Nopales* (page 103),
for serving

1 In a medium saucepan, bring the dried chiles and water to a boil over medium-high heat. Cover, reduce the heat to low, and simmer for 5 minutes until the chiles have softened. Remove from the heat and cool slightly.

2 Blend the chiles, 1 cup of their cooking water, orange juice, lime juice, onion, garlic, oregano, cumin, salt, and pepper in a blender until smooth.

3 Preheat the oven to 425°F. Lightly grease a large baking pan with cooking spray.

4 In the baking pan, combine the chicken and potatoes; season generously with salt and pepper. Pour the adobo sauce over the chicken and potatoes, making sure each piece is covered with adobo. Cover with aluminum foil.

5 Bake for 30 to 35 minutes. Uncover and bake for an additional 30 minutes. Serve with warm tortillas, *Arroz Mexicano*, and *Black Bean Salad with Corn and Nopales*.

TIP Substitute pineapple juice for the orange juice, and stir in 2 cups each of thinly sliced bell pepper and pineapple chunks for a fun and tropical twist.

CHICKEN & FISH

SALMÓN AL HORNO

In the early years of our marriage, my husband and I would splurge on salmon from time to time. I wanted simple baked salmon with butter, lemon, and garlic; he insisted on topping his with pico de gallo and avocado slices and eating it with tortillas. He insisted I try it. I was sure I wasn't going to like it, but I tried it anyway. Well, he was right, but I didn't mind one bit. Or bite!

Cooking spray
½ cup (1 stick) butter,
   at room temperature
2 garlic cloves, minced
2 tablespoons fresh
   lime juice
4 salmon fillets
Salt
Freshly ground black pepper
3 roma tomatoes, diced
½ medium red onion, diced
2 serrano chiles, seeded
   and diced
2 ripe avocados, diced
¼ cup finely chopped
   cilantro
Arroz blanco, for serving
Lemon wedges, for serving
Warmed flour tortillas,
   for serving

1 Preheat the oven to 350°F. Line a baking sheet with aluminum foil. Lightly grease the aluminum foil with cooking spray.

2 In a small bowl, mix together the softened butter, garlic, and lime juice.

3 Arrange the salmon fillets on the prepared baking sheet; season with salt and pepper. Brush the butter mixture all over the salmon.

4 Bake the salmon for 25 minutes, until the salmon flakes when tested with a fork.

5 While the salmon is baking, in a medium bowl, mix the tomatoes, onion, serrano chiles, avocado, and cilantro. Season with salt.

6 Remove the salmon from the oven. Top each fillet with avocado pico de gallo and season with pepper. Serve with arroz blanco, lemon wedges, and warm flour tortillas.

TIP *For the arroz blanco, prepare Poblano Rice (page 105), omitting the roasted poblano peppers and corn kernels.*

SALPICÓN DE POLLO

YIELD: 4 TO 6 SERVINGS   PREP TIME: 30 MINUTES

Salpicón is a classic Mexican salad traditionally made with shredded beef, but it can also be made with pork, fish, shrimp, and chicken. The fresh lime juice and olive oil combined with the onion, tomato, cilantro, and serrano chiles makes for a simple yet slightly tangy dressing. Salpicón de Pollo is a refreshing salad on its own, but when served inside a warm whole-wheat tortilla topped with diced avocado, it becomes a perfect meal for a hot summer day.

3 to 4 cups
   shredded chicken
3 roma tomatoes, chopped
2 serrano chiles, seeded
   and finely chopped
½ medium onion,
   finely chopped
1 garlic clove, minced
½ cup cilantro,
   finely chopped
¼ cup fresh lime juice
2 tablespoons olive oil
Salt
Freshly ground black pepper
½ head of iceberg lettuce,
   roughly chopped
2 ripe avocados, diced,
   for serving
Warmed whole-wheat
   tortillas, for serving

1 In a large bowl, mix together the chicken, tomatoes, chiles, onion, garlic, cilantro, lime juice, and olive oil. Season with salt and pepper. Cover with plastic wrap and refrigerate for 30 minutes before serving. Stir in the lettuce just before serving.

2 Garnish with avocado and serve with warm whole-wheat tortillas.

TIP *Substitute the chicken with 3 to 4 cups shredded imitation crab meat for a seafood favorite called* salpicón de jaiba.

TINGA DE POLLO

YIELD: 4 TO 6 SERVINGS   PREP TIME: 15 MINUTES   COOK TIME: 20 MINUTES

This is quite possibly the easiest recipe I have in my entire repertoire. It requires very little work and only a handful of ingredients, like shredded chicken, canned chipotles, and a simple homemade tomato sauce. It can be served on its own or as a filling for tacos and tostadas. I like to spoon a couple of tablespoons of shredded tinga de pollo atop round tortilla chips for a fun appetizer for a party or family get-together.

6 roma tomatoes
3 cups water
2 to 3 canned
    chipotles peppers
Salt
1 tablespoon vegetable oil
1 medium onion,
    thinly sliced
1 clove garlic, minced
3 to 4 cups shredded
    cooked chicken
Freshly ground black pepper
Arroz Mexicano (page 100),
    for serving
Refried Beans (page 96),
    for serving
Fresh green salad,
    for serving

1 In a medium saucepan, bring the tomatoes and water to a boil over medium-high heat. Cover, reduce the heat to low, and simmer for 5 to 10 minutes, until tomatoes are cooked through. Remove from the heat and cool slightly.

2 Blend the tomatoes with 1 cup of their cooking water and the chipotle peppers in a blender until smooth. Season with salt.

3 In a large nonstick skillet, heat the oil over medium-high heat. Add the onion and sauté for 2 to 3 minutes, until the onion turns translucent. Add the garlic and sauté for an additional 30 seconds. Stir in the shredded chicken and tomato purée and season with salt and pepper. Cover, reduce the heat to low, and simmer for 12 to 15 minutes, until the sauce has reduced slightly. Remove from the heat.

4 Serve with *Arroz Mexicano*, *Refried Beans*, and a fresh green salad. If serving as a filling for tacos and tostadas, garnish with shredded lettuce and crumbled queso fresco.

TIP *Stir in 3 roasted poblano peppers (cut into strips) for an added level of flavor.*

FISH & SEAFOOD
IN THE MEXICAN COCINA

Mexico loves fish and seafood in all forms. Shrimp, clams, oysters, scallops, octopus, catfish, trout, and red snapper are just a few of the vast array of the delicacies of the sea that are popular in Mexican cooking. There are restaurants known as marisquerías and pescaderías that specialize in serving only fish and seafood dishes. And let's not forget about the taquerías whose specialty are tacos de pescado. Classic Mexican dishes like caldo de pescado (fish soup), Veracruz-style fish, ceviche, and cóctel de camarón (shrimp cocktail) are some of the most popular menu items. Fresh fish and seafood are enjoyed year-round in Mexico, but are consumed most during Cuaresma (Lent), when it is customary for Mexican Catholics to refrain from eating red meat on Fridays.

As in every kitchen, cooking methods vary depending on the particular dish being prepared and the type of fish or seafood to be used.

Stewing is used to make soups and guisados like caldo de pescado, caldo de siete mares (soup of seven seas), Camarones a la Diabla (page 69), and also for cooking pulpo (octopus) to make it tender enough to use in other dishes like cóctel de camarón con pulpo.

An outdoor grill can be used to cook fish like salmon and fresh tuna a la parrilla, or with the help of a grill basket—sometimes called a zaranda in Spanish—to make Pescado Zarandeado (page 82). Wood-burning grills are also used to prepare crowd-pleasing dishes like Discada (page 50) and Pescado Dorado (page 84).

FIVE

RICE, BEANS & MORE

▽ ▽ ▽ ▽ ▽ ▽ ▽ ▽ ▽ ▽ ▽ ▽ ▽ ▽ ▽ ▽ ▽ ▽ ▽ ▽ ▽ ▽ ▽ ▽ ▽ ▽ ▽ ▽ ▽ ▽

No matter what kind of tacos you're craving, your meal wouldn't be complete without a few traditional Mexican side dishes. Classic Refried Beans (page 96) and Arroz Mexicano (page 100) are the perfect complement to any Mexican meal, but they aren't the only side dishes served in Mexican cocinas. This chapter is a collection of some of my family's favorite acompañamientos (side dishes), from my grandmother's creamy refried beans to cool and colorful salads made with black beans and nopales. I've also included recipes for Chiles Güeros Asados con Queso (page 104), Frijoles Borrachos (page 101), and how to make Frijoles de la Olla (page 95) using your slow cooker. Made with fresh ingredients, these side dishes—loaded with the comforting flavors and aromas of Mexican cuisine—are sure to delight your taste buds.

Many of the recipes included in this chapter can even be served on their own or as a filling for tacos. And best of all, they can be prepared in under 30 minutes without having to sacrifice flavor or authenticity.

RICE, BEANS & MORE

FRIJOLES DE LA OLLA

YIELD: 8 CUPS   PREP TIME: 10 MINUTES   COOK TIME: 6 TO 8 HOURS

Beans are the second most important ingredient in the Mexican diet (corn being the first). Frijoles de la Olla, "beans from the pot," are made in every Mexican cocina. Traditionally, frijoles de la olla are cooked on the stove top in a clay pot, but an easier way is let your slow cooker do all the work. I use pinto beans, but any kind of bean will work. Some favorites, besides pinto beans, are peruano beans, black beans, and flor de junio beans.

4 cups dried pinto beans
12 cups hot water
2 garlic cloves
1½ tablespoons salt
Chopped white onion,
    for garnish
Pinch dried Mexican
    oregano, for garnish

1 Sort the beans, separating out and discarding any rocks and other debris, then rinse with cold water in a colander.

2 In 6-quart slow cooker, mix the beans, hot water, and garlic. Cover and cook on the low-heat setting for 6 to 8 hours. Because beans and slow cookers vary, be sure to check the beans after 6 hours. When the beans are cooked through, remove from the heat and season with the salt.

3 Serve garnished with chopped white onion and a pinch dried Mexican oregano.

I always make a big batch of these beans and then freeze them for later. (If you're just making a few servings, divide this recipe by 4.) Cool the beans completely before storing in an airtight container in the refrigerator or freezer. They can be used as the base to traditional bean dishes like Refried Beans *(page 96) and* Frijoles Borrachos *(page 101).*

REFRIED BEANS

YIELD: 4 TO 6 SERVINGS   PREP TIME: 5 MINUTES   COOK TIME: 15 MINUTES

Frijoles refritos *(refried beans) were a constant at the dinner table when I was growing up. My grandmother made them every day of the week,* sin excepción *(without exception). And she always made a little extra for the* tacos de frijoles *she packed in my lunch every day for school.*

In Mexico, refried beans are traditionally made with manteca de cerdo, *but Gramm preferred to use bacon fat. She had a small canister on the stove where she saved any and all bacon drippings for just that purpose. Both bacon fat and manteca add tons of flavor, but if you're concerned about calories, vegetable oil works just as well.*

My grandmother's refried beans were as creamy as they were cheesy. That's because she always added a splash of milk and lots of shredded mozzarella cheese. Over the years, I've switched things up a little by substituting Mexican crema for the milk, which makes the beans even creamier, and using queso Oaxaca. I also like to add a little spice by sautéing a fresh serrano chile pepper in the bacon fat before adding the beans.

Refried beans aren't just a side dish; they can also be served for breakfast or as a filling for taquitos and tacos dorados.

2 to 3 tablespoons bacon drippings, manteca, or vegetable oil

1 fresh serrano chile (optional)

3 cups cooked pinto beans, canned or homemade

1½ cups bean broth (from dried beans cooking water or canned)

¼ cup Mexican crema or sour cream

Salt

1 cup shredded queso Oaxaca or mozzarella cheese

1 In a medium skillet, heat the bacon drippings over medium-high heat. Add the serrano chile (if using) and sauté for 1 minute, until its skin begins to blister. Add the cooked beans, bean broth, and Mexican crema and bring to a boil. Using a potato masher, mash the beans to the desired consistency. Season with salt.

2 Continue cooking the beans for 5 to 8 minutes, stirring constantly, until the beans thicken slightly. Remove from the heat and stir in the cheese.

TIP *Substitute 1 whole dried chipotle chile for the serrano chile for refried beans with an intense smoky and spicy flavor.*

FRIJOLES ADOBADOS

YIELD: 6 SERVINGS   PREP TIME: 15 MINUTES   COOK TIME: 30 MINUTES

Frijoles adobados *are a spicy and hearty dish of cooked beans simmered in a flavorful adobo made with dried chiles and spices. The adobo can vary in flavor from super spicy to semisweet. For me, it really depends on what kind of bean I'm using. With black beans, I prefer a rich, dark, and flavorful adobo made with whatever is in my spice cabinet, like cumin, paprika, oregano, saffron, and instant coffee granules for a semisweet, almost mole-like adobo.*

3 dried pasilla chiles, stemmed and seeded

2 dried guajillo chiles, stemmed and seeded

1 dried chipotle pepper, stemmed

3 cups water

½ medium white onion, chopped

2 garlic cloves, minced

2 tablespoons vegetable oil

6 ounces Mexican *Pork Chorizo* (page 56) or store-bought (casings removed)

4 cups cooked black beans, drained and rinsed

2 tablespoons brown sugar

1 tablespoon instant coffee granules

1 teaspoon salt

½ teaspoon ground cumin

½ teaspoon paprika

½ teaspoon Mexican oregano

¼ teaspoon black pepper

⅛ teaspoon saffron

½ cup cilantro leaves

Lime wedges, for garnish

1 In a medium saucepan, bring the dried chiles, pepper, and water to a boil over high heat. Cover, reduce the heat to low, and simmer for about 5 minutes, until the chiles have softened completely. Remove from the heat and cool slightly.

2 Blend the chiles, their cooking water, the onion, and the garlic in a blender until smooth.

3 In a large skillet, heat the oil over medium-high heat. Add the chorizo and cook, breaking it up into small pieces using the back of a wooden spoon, for 6 to 8 minutes, until fully cooked but not completely browned. Stir in the beans, chile purée, brown sugar, coffee granules, salt, cumin, paprika, oregano, pepper, and saffron, and cook, stirring occasionally, for 6 to 8 minutes, until the beans start to boil. Reduce the heat to low. Using a potato masher, lightly mash the black beans to the desired consistency. Simmer, stirring occasionally, for 12 to 15 minutes, then remove from the heat.

4 Garnish the beans with fresh cilantro leaves and lime wedges. Serve over white rice for a delicious and easy meal, or as a side dish with *Carnitas* (page 45), *Cochinita Pibil* (page 52), or your favorite seafood tacos.

TIP A tasty twist to this recipe is to prepare it with pinto beans and substitute the dried pasilla chiles with dried ancho chiles.

ARROZ MEXICANO

YIELD: 6 SERVINGS   PREP TIME: 5 MINUTES   COOK TIME: 25 MINUTES

In Mexico, recipes for Arroz Mexicano (Mexican rice)—also known as sopa de arroz—vary from region to region, and even family to family. This family recipe is one I hold near and dear to my heart because it was one of the first recipes my suegra shared with me during her first visit to the United States, which also happened to be my first time meeting her.

3 roma tomatoes, quartered
½ medium onion
1 garlic clove
2½ cups chicken broth
3 tablespoons vegetable oil
1 cup long-grain rice
Salt

1 In a blender, add the tomatoes, onion, garlic, and chicken broth, and blend until smooth.

2 In a large skillet, heat the oil over medium-high heat. Add the rice and sauté, stirring constantly, for 8 to 10 minutes, until light golden brown.

3 Carefully pour in the tomato purée, stirring gently to combine. Season with salt. No stirring beyond this point!

4 Cover and bring to a boil. Reduce the heat to low and simmer for 15 to 20 minutes, until all the liquid is absorbed. Remove from the heat and let the rice set for at least 5 minutes before serving.

TIP *Add a hint of color by stirring in 1 (8-ounce) can of golden corn kernels (drained); 1 medium carrot, finely chopped; and/or 1 cup of frozen peas in step 3 with the tomato purée.*

FRIJOLES BORRACHOS

YIELD: 8 TO 10 SERVINGS   PREP TIME: 10 MINUTES   COOK TIME: 35 MINUTES

Frijoles Borrachos (drunken beans) are a fun way to liven up cooked beans. Made with bacon, fresh chiles, spices, and beer, they are the perfect side dish to serve at your next get-together with family and friends.

1 tablespoon vegetable oil

4 bacon slices, cut into 1-inch pieces

1 medium onion, finely chopped

2 fresh serrano chiles, finely chopped

2 garlic cloves, minced

3 large roma tomatoes, diced

6 cups cooked pinto beans (*Frijoles de la Olla*, page 95)

3 cups bean or chicken broth

1 (12-ounce) bottle dark Mexican beer

4 cilantro sprigs

1 teaspoon salt

½ teaspoon ground cumin

¼ teaspoon Mexican oregano

Mexican crema, for garnish

Grated queso asadero, or Monterey Jack or provolone cheeses, for garnish

Warmed corn tortillas, for serving

1 In a Dutch oven, heat the oil over medium-high heat. Add the bacon and cook for 3 to 5 minutes, until lightly browned.

2 Add the onion, serrano chiles, and garlic, and cook, stirring occasionally, for 1 to 2 minutes, until the onion turns translucent.

3 Add the tomatoes and cook for another 2 to 3 minutes. Add the beans, bean broth, beer, and cilantro. Season with the salt, cumin, and oregano. Cover and bring to a boil. Lightly mash the beans with potato masher to help thicken the broth. Reduce the heat to low and simmer for 15 to 20 minutes.

4 Ladle into bowls and top with a dollop of Mexican crema and grated queso asadero. Serve with warm corn tortillas.

TIP Frijoles Borrachos *can also be served as a stew. Ladle into bowls and top with a dollop of Mexican* crema *and grated* asadero *cheese. Serve with warm corn tortillas.*

ENSALADA DE NOPALES

YIELD: 4 TO 6 SERVINGS   PREP TIME: 10 MINUTES   COOK TIME: 20 MINUTES

This colorful cactus paddle salad is the perfect side dish for traditional Mexican dishes, but is a delicious garnish for tacos as well. On hot summer days, a simple corn-tortilla taco filled with ensalada de nopales is a cool and refreshing light lunch.

1 pound nopales, cleaned and thinly sliced or roughly chopped (see recipe tip, below, and "Fresh Nopales 101," page 107)

Coarse salt

3 roma tomatoes, chopped

½ medium onion, chopped

1 fresh serrano chile, seeded and finely chopped (optional)

3 tablespoons finely chopped cilantro

1 In a medium nonstick skillet, place the nopales and season lightly with coarse salt. Cover the skillet and simmer over low heat. Within minutes the nopales will start to release their liquid and cook in it. Continue to simmer over low heat, stirring occasionally, until all the liquid is absorbed and the nopales are cooked through with very little to no cactus "slime" whatsoever. Let cool completely.

2 In a medium bowl, gently mix together the cooked nopales, tomatoes, onion, serrano chile (if using), and cilantro. Season lightly with salt. Serve as a side dish or as a topping for your favorite tacos.

TIP *If you are unable to find fresh nopales at the grocery store, substitute 1 (30-ounce) can or jar of nopales. Drain the nopales and rinse with cold water before mixing into the salad.*

BLACK BEAN SALAD WITH CORN AND NOPALES

YIELD: 6 TO 8 SERVINGS   PREP TIME: 10 MINUTES   COOK TIME: 60 MINUTES

This refreshing black bean salad is ideal for summer cookouts in the backyard. Packed with a colorful mix of black beans, tomatoes, golden corn kernels, nopales, and queso panela seasoned with cilantro, fresh chiles, and lime juice, this salad can be served on its own as a light meal, in a whole-wheat tortilla wrap, as a dip with tortilla chips, or as a side dish with your favorite tacos.

3½ cups cooked black beans, drained

3 roma tomatoes, finely chopped

½ medium red onion, finely chopped

2 serrano chiles, seeded and finely chopped

1 garlic clove, minced

1 (12-ounce) can golden corn kernels, drained

1½ cups cooked nopales (see step 1 of *Ensalada de Nopales*, page 102, for technique), roughly chopped

¼ cup chopped cilantro

3 limes, halved

¼ teaspoon ground cumin

Salt

Freshly ground black pepper

1 cup crumbled queso panela

1 In a large bowl, mix together the black beans, tomatoes, red onion, serrano chiles, garlic, corn, nopales, and cilantro. Squeeze the juice of the limes over and mix gently to combine. Season with ground cumin, salt, and pepper.

2 Cover the bowl with plastic wrap and refrigerate for at least 1 hour before serving. Stir in the crumbled queso panela just before serving.

TIP For an interesting twist, replace half of the black beans with cooked pinto or peruano beans. Peruano beans are pale yellow in color, have a mild buttery flavor, and are soft and creamy in texture.

CHILES GÜEROS ASADOS CON QUESO

∨∨∨∨∨∨∨∨∨ ∨∨∨∨∨∨ ∨∨∨∨∨∨∨∨ ∨∨∨∨∨∨ ∨∨∨∨∨∨∨∨ ∨∨∨∨∨∨∨∨

YIELD: 12 CHILES   PREP TIME: 5 MINUTES   COOK TIME: 15 MINUTES

Whenever we fire up the grill for a carne asada with family and friends, there are a few classic sides that we always include on the grill: green onions, whole cactus paddles topped with queso fresco, and these yellow chiles stuffed with cheese. Slow roasted over a low flame, the chiles güeros soften as they cook, while the cheese melts inside, creating a spicy, mouthwatering stuffed chile.

12 yellow (güero) chiles
2 ¼ cups shredded queso
　Oaxaca or queso fresco

1 Slice the yellow chiles open without cutting through to the other side. Scoop out the seeds and veins using a small spoon. Stuff each chile with 2 to 3 tablespoons of shredded cheese. Secure chiles with a toothpick, if desired.

2 Preheat the grill. Roast the chiles on a grill directly over a low flame for 10 to 12 minutes, turning occasionally, until the chiles begin to char. The chiles can also be roasted on a comal over low heat on the stove top.

TIP *Experiment with other chiles like Hatch, Anaheim, and even fresh jalapeños for different heat levels and taste profiles.*

POBLANO RICE

This dish has all the flavor of Rajas con Crema *(page 125) in a delicious side dish. Roasted poblano peppers and golden corn kernels are a classic flavor combination (and an all-time favorite of mine) that adds tons of flavor and a splash of bright color to any dish. Poblano rice pairs nicely with grilled meats and pork carnitas.*

2 fresh poblano chiles
½ medium white
  onion, chopped
1 garlic clove, minced
2½ cups chicken broth
2 tablespoons vegetable oil
1 cup long-grain rice
1 cup (canned) golden corn
  kernels, drained
¼ teaspoon salt

TIP *Love a good cheesy rice dish? Stir in 1½ cups shredded queso manchego or queso asadero once you've turned off the heat.*

1 Heat a comal, griddle, or nonstick skillet over high heat. Toast the poblano chiles, turning occasionally, until the skin is completely charred. Transfer the chiles to a plastic or paper bag and set the chiles aside for at least 5 minutes. Using your fingers or a paper towel, peel the blistered skin off of the chiles.

2 Slice off the stems, remove the seeds and veins with a spoon, and roughly dice the roasted chiles.

3 Blend the onion, garlic, and chicken broth in a blender until smooth.

4 In a large skillet, heat the oil over medium-high heat. Add the rice and sauté until light golden brown, about 4 minutes. Add the diced poblano peppers and corn kernels, and cook, stirring occasionally, for 1 to 2 minutes. Carefully pour in the onion purée, stirring gently to combine, and season with the salt. Do not stir beyond this point!

5 Cover and bring the rice to a boil. Reduce the heat to low and simmer for 15 to 20 minutes, until all the liquid has been absorbed.

DAIRY FREE

RICE, BEANS & MORE

SOPA DE FIDEO SECO

YIELD: 4 TO 6 SERVINGS PREP TIME: 5 MINUTES COOK TIME: 20 MINUTES

Sopa de Fideo Seco is a classic Mexican dish that goes nicely with refried beans and your favorite guisado or as a filling for tacos. Kids love it! My grandmother prepared different versions of this sopa *(often referred to as Mexican spaghetti) every day of the week by simply varying the type of pasta used. Try it with elbow macaroni, shells, penne, stars, and alphabet pasta.*

3 roma tomatoes, quartered
¼ medium onion, chopped
1 garlic clove, minced
2½ cups chicken broth
2 tablespoons vegetable oil
1½ cups dried fideo pasta
   (vermicelli)
Salt
1 cup shredded queso
   Chihuahua or
   queso Oaxaca

1 Blend the tomatoes, onion, garlic, and chicken broth in a blender until smooth.

2 In a large skillet, heat the oil over medium-high heat. Add the pasta and sauté, stirring constantly to prevent the noodles from burning, for 5 to 7 minutes, until the noodles turn golden brown.

3 Carefully pour in the tomato purée, stirring gently to combine. Season lightly with salt. Cover the skillet and bring to a boil. Reduce the heat to low and simmer until all the liquid is absorbed.

4 Remove from the heat. Sprinkle shredded cheese over the fideo. Cover and let sit for about 5 minutes, allowing the cheese to melt.

TIP *To make the soupier version of this pasta dish (Sopa de Fideo), increase the chicken broth or water to 8 cups and omit the cheese.*

TAQUERÍA TACOS

FRESH NOPALES 101

Nopales are the leaves, also called cactus paddles, of the prickly pear cactus and are a vegetable popular in Mexican cuisine. Loaded with vitamins, minerals, and antioxidants, adding cactus paddles to your diet can help lower glucose and cholesterol levels. Did I mention they're also incredibly delicious?

When cleaning the cactus paddles, always start at the base as it is sturdier than the tip. Holding the base of the cactus paddle with kitchen tongs, take a sharp kitchen knife and scrape away the espinas (thorns) from the bottom to the top, then turn the cactus leaf over and repeat on the other side. You also want to trim off the outer edge of the cactus paddle as it can be tougher and more fibrous than the rest of the paddle. Rinse the paddles with cold water and a kitchen brush to remove any stray thorns. Practice makes perfect when it comes to cleaning nopales, and even the most experienced cooks get stuck with a couple of thorns in their hands. The thorns are bothersome, but easily removed with tweezers.

SIX

VEGETABLES

▽ ▽

Vegetables play an important role in Mexican cooking, whether they are added to soups, stews, or guisados or served as a main dish. Fresh vegetables like chiles, corn, nopales, potatoes, onions, green beans, carrots, chayotes, calabacitas, and squash blossoms are all very popular in Mexican cooking.

In this chapter, I share comforting dishes from my childhood like Camotes Enmielados *(candied sweet potatoes; page 113)*, Papas con Chorizo *(potatoes with chorizo; page 121), and* Calabacitas *(a colorful zucchini medley of veggies; page 111).*

I've also included some of my family's grilled favorites, like Grilled Corn con Limón y Chile *(page 120)*, Cebollitas Asadas *(grilled onions; page 114)*, Nopales Asados con Queso *(grilled cactus paddles with cheese; page 122), and* Champiñones Rellenos Asados *(queso fresco–stuffed mushrooms; page 116).*

And then there are a few double-duty recipes like Papas con Rajas *(page 124)*, Calabacitas con Crema *(page 112)*, Espinacas con Queso *(page 119), and* Rajas con Crema *(page 125) that can be served either as a side dish or as a filling for tacos and quesadillas.*

VEGETABLES

CALABACITAS

YIELD: 4 TO 6 SERVINGS   PREP TIME: 10 MINUTES   COOK TIME: 25 MINUTES

A classic Mexican comfort dish, guisado de calabacitas was the only way my grandmother ever cooked zucchini or Mexican calabacitas. A bright and colorful vegetable side dish made with tomato, onion, corn, and queso fresco, calabacitas are an excellent year-round treat. They are great at a summer cookout with friends, as one of the many side dishes on your Thanksgiving table, or stuffed inside a warm tortilla for a light lunch or dinner.

2 tablespoons vegetable oil
½ medium white
  onion, diced
2 serrano chiles, seeded and
  thinly sliced
1 garlic clove, minced
1 pound Mexican
  calabacitas or zucchini,
  cut into 1-inch slices
3 roma tomatoes, diced
1½ cups (canned) golden
  corn kernels, drained
Salt
Freshly ground black pepper
1 cup crumbled queso cotija
  or queso fresco

1 In a large skillet, heat the oil over medium-high heat. Add the onion and serrano chiles and sauté for 2 to 3 minutes, until the onion is translucent. Add the garlic and sauté for an additional 30 seconds. Add the calabacitas, tomatoes, and corn, and season with salt and pepper.

2 Cover, reduce the heat to low, and simmer for 2 to 15 minutes until the calabacitas are cooked through. Remove from the heat and sprinkle with queso cotija just before serving.

TIP *This recipe can also be made with shredded cabbage in place of the calabacitas. Substitute queso Chihuahua for the crumbled cotija.*

CALABACITAS CON CREMA

YIELD: 6 TO 8 SERVINGS   PREP TIME: 5 MINUTES   COOK TIME: 25 MINUTES

Calabacitas con Crema *is one of my favorite side dishes because it is a delicious combination of two Mexican classics: guisado de calabacitas and* Rajas con Crema *(page 125). Made with Mexican calabacitas or zucchini, golden corn kernels, serrano chile, and Mexican crema, calabacitas con crema can be served as a side dish with spicy red guisados to help tone down the heat or as a filling for tacos, quesadillas, and even empanadas for* Cuaresma *(Lent). To make the sauce even richer, I like to add a little cream cheese.*

2 tablespoons butter

½ medium onion, finely chopped

2 serrano chiles, seeded and finely chopped

1 garlic clove, minced

1 cup Mexican crema or sour cream

3 ounces cream cheese, softened

Salt

Freshly ground black pepper

2 pounds Mexican calabacitas or zucchini, cut into bite-size pieces

2 cups corn kernels, drained or defrosted

¼ to ½ cup milk (optional)

1 In a large skillet, melt the butter over high heat. Add the onion and serrano chiles and sauté, stirring occasionally, for 2 to 3 minutes, until the onion turns translucent. Add the garlic and sauté for an additional 30 seconds.

2 Using a wooden spoon or wire whisk, stir in the Mexican crema and cream cheese until combined, then season generously with salt and pepper.

3 Add the calabacitas and corn and reduce the heat to low. Cover the skillet and simmer for 15 to 20 minutes, stirring occasionally, until the calabacitas are tender. Remove from the heat. If the sauce gets too thick while simmering, stir in ¼ cup of milk (if using), adding more as necessary.

TIP *Add an intense smoky flavor to this dish by substituting 2 finely chopped canned chipotles in adobo sauce for the serrano chiles.*

CAMOTES ENMIELADOS

YIELD: 4 TO 6 SERVINGS   PREP TIME: 10 MINUTES   COOK TIME: 50 MINUTES

A comforting dessert, Camotes Enmielados *reminds me of my childhood. Gramm prepared her candied sweet potatoes for holidays like Thanksgiving, Christmas, and New Year's, while Pappy made them on cold, gloomy days. Thick slices of sweet potato are simmered over low heat in a rich syrup made from* piloncillo *(unrefined sugar shaped into cones) and cinnamon that enhances the natural sweetness of the sweet potatoes.*

2 pounds sweet potatoes
   or yams, cut into
   1½-inch slices

1½ cups water

2 dark piloncillo cones,
   or 2 cups dark brown
   sugar plus 2 tablespoons
   molasses

2 cinnamon sticks

Warm milk, for serving

Sweetened condensed milk,
   for serving

1 In a Dutch oven, arrange the sweet potato slices. Pour the water over the sweet potatoes. Arrange the piloncillo cones and cinnamon sticks on top of the sweet potatoes. Cover and simmer over low heat for 45 to 50 minutes, until the sweet potatoes are cooked through and the syrup has thickened. (Resist the urge to stir as this will break up the sweet potatoes and turn them into mush.)

2 Serve warm with milk or drizzle a little sweetened condensed milk on top.

 Substitute a small 4-pound pumpkin (cut into 2-inch pieces) for the sweet potatoes to make calabaza en tacha, *a traditional pumpkin dessert served on* Día de Muertos *(Day of the Dead) and during the cold autumn and winter months. Also, I encourage you to stick to dark (and not light) piloncillo cones for this recipe. Dark piloncillo results in a thick, rich syrup for the sweet potatoes, while light piloncillo would result in a thin, watery syrup (not good!).*

CEBOLLITAS ASADAS

YIELD: 4 TO 6 SERVINGS   PREP TIME: 5 MINUTES   COOK TIME: 30 MINUTES

No matter what we're grilling at the family ranch, our cookouts wouldn't be complete without a few grilled onions. Make that a lot of grilled onions. Drizzled with olive oil and seasoned with coarse salt, grilled onions taste best when slightly charred on the outside and sweet and tender on the inside. They're so good, we're always sure to make extra because they're the first to disappear and are perfect for serving alongside grilled meats.

4 medium white onions, peeled and cut into 6 to 8 wedges

2 tablespoons olive oil or vegetable oil

½ teaspoon coarse salt

1 Preheat the grill to medium-low heat.

2 Arrange the onion wedges in the center of a 32x18-inch piece of aluminum foil. Drizzle the olive oil over the onion wedges and season with the salt. Wrap the onions tightly in the aluminum foil.

3 Grill, turning occasionally, for 25 to 30 minutes, until the onions are tender and the skin has begun to char.

 Add a little spice by adding 1 whole chile güero to the package before grilling.

CHAMPIÑONES CON RAJAS

YIELD: 4 TO 6 SERVINGS   PREP TIME: 15 MINUTES   COOK TIME: 15 MINUTES

This delicious dish of mushrooms and roasted poblano pepper strips, with its contrasting spicy and earthy flavors, can be served as a side dish with Carne Asada *(page 43) or other grilled meats and seafood, on its own with toast or crackers for a light lunch, or as a meatless filling for tacos and quesadillas. During the rainy season, I use the wild* hongos *(mushrooms) my husband and the kiddies find in the fields, but any kind of fresh mushroom will do just fine in this recipe.*

3 poblano chiles
2 tablespoons vegetable oil
½ medium white
   onion, sliced
1 serrano chile, seeded and
   finely chopped
1 pound mushrooms, sliced
2 roma tomatoes, diced
1 garlic clove, minced
Salt
Freshly ground black pepper
Crumbled queso fresco
   (optional)

1 Heat a comal, griddle, or nonstick skillet over medium-high heat. Add the poblano chiles and roast, turning occasionally, until the skin is completely charred. Put the chiles in a plastic or paper bag and let sit for at least 5 minutes. Using your fingers or a paper towel, peel the charred skin from the peppers. Remove the stems and seeds, and roughly chop the peppers. Set aside.

2 In a large skillet, heat the oil over medium-high heat. Add the sliced onion and serrano chile and sauté, stirring occasionally, for 2 to 3 minutes, until the onions turn translucent.

3 Add the chopped roasted poblano chiles, mushrooms, tomatoes, and garlic, and season with salt and pepper. Reduce the heat to low and simmer, stirring occasionally, for 10 to 12 minutes. Remove from the heat and sprinkle with crumbled queso fresco.

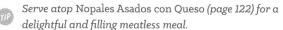 *Serve atop* Nopales Asados con Queso *(page 122) for a delightful and filling meatless meal.*

CHAMPIÑONES RELLENOS ASADOS

YIELD: 4 TO 6 SERVINGS   PREP TIME: 10 MINUTES   COOK TIME: 15 MINUTES

These queso fresco–stuffed mushrooms are another of our must-have dishes at el rancho with family and friends, no matter what we're cooking on the grill or in the clay oven. Champiñones Rellenos Asados *can be served as a side dish with grilled or roasted meats or as an appetizer. Try it with* Carne Asada *(page 43),* Pescado Zarandeado *(page 82), or* Pollo Adobado *(page 86).*

½ pound cremini mushrooms, stems removed and reserved

Salt

5 ounces queso fresco, crumbled

1 serrano chile, seeded and finely chopped

1 tablespoon finely chopped cilantro

1 Preheat the grill over a low flame.

2 Wipe the mushrooms with a paper towel to clean off any excess dirt. Sprinkle the insides with salt. Set aside.

3 Finely chop the mushroom stems.

4 In a small bowl, mix together the queso fresco, serrano chile, cilantro, and mushroom stems until well combined.

5 Fill each mushroom cap with heaping tablespoons of the queso fresco mixture.

6 Grill the stuffed mushrooms over a low flame for about 10 minutes, until the cheese starts to bubble.

TIP *You can still make thes mushroom bites without a grill. Bake them on an ungreased baking sheet at 350°F for 10 to 12 minutes.*

EJOTES EN CHILE COLORADO

DAIRY FREE

YIELD: 4 TO 6 SERVINGS   PREP TIME: 15 MINUTES   COOK TIME: 30 MINUTES

Pappy loved adding chile colorado to absolutely everything. He added it to eggs, soups and stews, and even vegetables like green beans for a delectable side dish. Dried chiles weren't as readily available as they are now, so Pappy made this dish with canned enchilada sauce. For this recipe, you'll see how easy it is to make your own sauce. Serve with Carnitas *(page 45) or* Carne Asada *(page 43) and* Arroz Mexicano *(page 100).*

8 cups water, divided
1 pound green beans
2 teaspoons salt, plus more for seasoning
3 dried ancho chiles, stemmed and seeded
1 garlic clove, minced
1 tablespoon masa harina
¼ teaspoon ground cumin
¼ teaspoon crushed Mexican oregano
1 to 2 tablespoons lard or vegetable oil
¼ medium onion, finely chopped

1 In a large pot, bring 6 cups of the water to a boil over high heat. Add the green beans and salt and cook for 6 to 8 minutes until tender. Drain and set aside.

2 In a small saucepan, bring the remaining 2 cups of the water and dried chiles to a boil over medium-high heat. Remove from the heat, cover the saucepan, and let sit for 5 minutes until the chiles are softened.

3 Blend the chiles, their cooking water, the garlic, masa harina, cumin, and oregano in a blender until smooth.

4 In a large skillet, heat the lard over medium-high heat. Add the onion and sauté, stirring occasionally, for 2 to 3 minutes, until the onion is translucent. Add the chile purée, stirring to combine, and season with salt. Add the drained green beans and stir. Cover the skillet, reduce the heat to low, and simmer for 15 minutes.

TIP
Substitute 1 (10-ounce) can of red enchilada sauce for the homemade sauce.

ENSALADA DE BETABEL

YIELD: 4 TO 6 SERVINGS   PREP TIME: 15 MINUTES

I was one of those weird kids who loved vegetables (with the exception of nopales). You name it, I liked it. Spinach, Brussels sprouts, cabbage . . . I liked them all. I even liked beets! It wasn't until I moved to Mexico that I discovered that this beloved vegetable I had only eaten cooked could also be enjoyed raw. Seasoned with fresh lime juice and Tajín, this salad is fresh, slightly tart, and perfect for any outdoor fiesta.

1½ cups shredded raw beets
1½ cups shredded
   raw carrots
1½ cups shredded
   raw jicama
¼ cup freshly squeezed
   lime juice
1 teaspoon Tajín seasoning
   or ground chile
Salt

In a large bowl, combine the beets, carrots, and jicama. Add the lime juice, Tajín seasoning, and some salt, then toss. Serve immediately. Refrigerate any leftovers in an airtight container.

Add more color to this vibrant salad by adding shredded mango and/or peeled and shredded cucumber.

ESPINACAS CON QUESO

YIELD: 4 TO 6 SERVINGS   PREP TIME: 5 MINUTES   COOK TIME: 15 MINUTES

Gramm loved to tell the story of how as a baby all I wanted to eat were jars of puréed spinach and that I turned up my nose at everything else. Well, a few decades have passed since then, but spinach continues to be one of my favorite veggies. This simple dish of sautéed spinach with bacon and queso fresco can be served as a side dish or as a filling for quick and easy Tacos de Espinacas con Queso.

4 bacon slices, roughly chopped
½ medium onion, finely chopped
1 garlic clove, minced
10 to 12 ounces fresh baby spinach
Salt
1½ cups crumbled queso fresco

1 In a large nonstick skillet, cook the bacon over medium-high heat until lightly crisp. Drain all but 1 tablespoon of the bacon grease from the pan.

2 Add the onion and sauté for 2 to 3 minutes, until the onion turns translucent. Add garlic and sauté for an additional 30 seconds. Add the spinach and stir. Season with salt and cook, stirring occasionally, for 3 to 5 minutes, until the spinach starts to wilt. Remove from the heat.

3 Sprinkle the cheese over the spinach. Cover the skillet and let sit for 5 minutes before serving.

TIP *Stir* Espinacas con Queso *into cooked pasta for an easy weeknight dinner.*

VEGETABLES

119

GRILLED CORN CON LIMÓN Y CHILE

YIELD: 6 SERVINGS   PREP TIME: 5 MINUTES   COOK TIME: 20 MINUTES

Our favorite time to visit the ranch is toward the end of the rainy season. Everything is green and lush, and the corn my brother-in-law planted a few months earlier is ripe for harvesting. Grilling corn might sound simple enough, but the secret to a juicy cob of corn is to leave the husks on. The corn husks dry out and end up completely charred, but inside the corn kernels are steaming to sweet perfection.

6 ears fresh corn,
  with husks
6 limes, cut into wedges
Tajín or chile powder, for
  seasoning

1 Preheat the grill to a medium-high flame.

2 Arrange the corn on the grill. Cover and grill, turning occasionally, for 15 to 18 minutes, until the husks are charred. Remove from the heat and cool for about 5 minutes. Carefully pull back the charred husks and discard.

3 If serving a crowd, cut each ear of corn into 3 or 4 pieces. Squeeze lime juice over the corn and sprinkle with Tajín seasoning.

 For traditional Mexican street corn, spread mayonnaise or Mexican crema over cooked corn and sprinkle with crumbled queso cotija.

TAQUERÍA TACOS

PAPAS CON CHORIZO

YIELD: 4 TO 6 SERVINGS   PREP TIME: 5 MINUTES   COOK TIME: 30 MINUTES

Papas con Chorizo is a comfort food classic often served for breakfast alongside refried beans and a fried egg or as a filling for tacos and burritos. Whenever I boil potatoes to make Tacos Dorados de Papa *(page 174), I always add a few extra to have on hand. This recipe's base is fried potatoes with chorizo, but you can enhance the flavors by adding ingredients like tomatoes, green chiles, or nopales.*

2 tablespoons vegetable oil

½ pound Mexican *Pork Chorizo* (homemade, page 56, or store-bought, casing removed)

½ medium onion, finely chopped

1 banana pepper, seeded and finely chopped (optional)

4 medium potatoes, boiled, peeled, and diced

2 roma tomatoes, finely chopped

Salt

Freshly ground black pepper

Refried Beans (page 96), for serving

1 In a large nonstick skillet or Dutch oven, heat the oil over medium-high heat. Add the chorizo to the skillet, using the back of a wooden spoon to break it up, and cook, for 8 to 10 minutes, or until cooked through and lightly browned. Using a slotted spoon, transfer the chorizo to a heat-proof plate. Add the onion and banana pepper to the skillet and sauté, stirring occasionally, for 2 to 3 minutes, until the onion turns translucent.

2 Stir in the potatoes and fry for 3 to 5 minutes, until lightly browned. Add the tomatoes and cooked chorizo, and season with salt and pepper. Cover, reduce the heat to medium-low, and simmer, stirring occasionally, for 10 to 12 minutes. Serve with *Refried Beans*.

TIP *For a hearty Mexican breakfast, top each serving with a fried egg and your favorite salsa.*

NOPALES ASADOS CON QUESO

YIELD: 4 TO 6 SERVINGS   PREP TIME: 5 MINUTES   COOK TIME: 25 MINUTES

Nopales are one of the most popular vegetables in the Mexican cocina—and with good reason. With their light and zesty flavor, nopales are absolutely delicious and packed with vitamins and minerals. They can be boiled, sautéed, baked, and grilled. They can be added to soups, salads, and pretty much any type of guisado, and they can also be enjoyed entirely on their own.

That said, I wasn't always a fan of nopales. I remember Pappy always had a jar of nopalitos in the refrigerator and another in the pantry, because they reminded him of his childhood in the small rural community Villa Matamoros, Chihuahua, Mexico. No matter how Gramm and Pappy prepared them, I refused to try nopales because I couldn't stomach ingesting the babas (the slime-like liquid nopales produce as they cook). When we moved to Mexico, I discovered grilling nopales over an open flame eliminates most of the babas. One taste and I was hooked for life. Once you try these grilled nopales with queso fresco, you'll understand why. And you don't need a grill to enjoy this Mexican delicacy. I make these in the oven more often than I do out on the grill.

Cooking spray
2 pounds nopales; medium to small paddles are best
Salt
10 ounces queso fresco, sliced

1 Preheat the oven to 425°F. Lightly grease a baking sheet with cooking spray.

2 Arrange the cactus paddles on the baking sheet and season lightly with salt.

3 Bake the cactus paddles for 7 to 10 minutes. Turn the cactus paddles over, season lightly again with salt, and bake for 5 to 7 minutes more. You'll know the nopales are done when they have darkened in color and are soft and pliable like a tortilla.

4 Top each paddle with 1 or 2 slices of the cheese. Bake for an additional 3 to 5 minutes, until the cheese starts to bubble.

TIP *Make* Nopales Asados *on the stove top by roasting cactus paddles on a comal or griddle over low heat.*

PAPAS CON RAJAS

YIELD: 4 TO 6 SERVINGS   PREP TIME: 10 MINUTES   COOK TIME: 25 MINUTES

Papas con Rajas *is a tasty dish made with golden fried potatoes, onion, and three types of roasted green chiles. Serve for breakfast (with a fried egg on top) or as a side dish with grilled meats. It has long been one of my go-to meatless fillings for tacos and burritos when we're running low on groceries or when the budget is tight, though it goes well with grilled and roasted meats, too.*

2 poblano peppers
2 Anaheim chiles
2 banana peppers
1 tablespoon butter
1 tablespoon vegetable oil
½ medium onion,
   roughly chopped
4 medium potatoes, boiled,
   peeled, and diced
1 garlic clove, minced
Salt
Freshly ground black pepper

1 Heat a comal, griddle, or nonstick skillet over medium-high heat. Roast the poblano peppers, Anaheim chiles, and banana peppers, turning occasionally, until completely charred. Transfer to a plastic or paper bag and let sit for at least 5 minutes. Using your fingers or paper towels, peel off the charred skin. Remove the stems and seeds and roughly chop the peppers and chiles. Set aside.

2 In a large skillet, heat the butter and oil over high heat until the butter melts. Add the onion and sauté, stirring occasionally, for 2 to 3 minutes, until translucent. Add the potatoes and cook, stirring occasionally, for 3 to 5 minutes, until lightly browned.

3 Stir in the garlic and roasted chiles and season with salt and pepper. Cover the skillet, reduce the heat to low, and simmer for 10 minutes, stirring occasionally. Remove from the heat. Serve with grilled or roasted meats.

For a fun and tasty twist, try substituting sweet potatoes for the potatoes.

RAJAS CON CREMA

YIELD: 4 TO 6 SERVINGS   PREP TIME: 10 MINUTES   COOK TIME: 20 MINUTES

I grew up eating Pappy's Chile de Rajas con Queso *(page 134) as a salsa for everything from eggs to grilled meats and quesadillas, but I was pleasantly surprised when my suegra made a creamier version and served it as a main dish for a Viernes de Cuaresma (Lent Friday). Turns out that my suegra hadn't made chile de rajas at all, but a classic meatless dish called rajas con crema, which is simply strips of roasted poblano chiles swimming in Mexican crema.*

8 poblano peppers
1 to 2 tablespoons
    vegetable oil
1 medium onion, sliced
2 garlic cloves, minced
3 roma tomatoes, diced
2 cups Mexican crema or
    sour cream
Salt
Freshly ground black pepper
Arroz Mexicano (page 100)
Refried Beans (page 96)

1 Heat a comal, griddle, or nonstick skillet over medium-high heat. Roast the poblano peppers, turning occasionally, until charred. Transfer the roasted peppers to a plastic or paper bag and let sit for at least 5 minutes. Using your fingers or paper towels, peel off the charred skin. Remove the stems and seeds and slice the peppers into thin strips. Set aside.

2 In a large skillet, heat the oil over high heat. Add the onion and sauté for 2 to 3 minutes, stirring occasionally, until it turns translucent. Add the garlic and sauté for an additional 30 seconds.

3 Stir in the roasted poblano strips, tomatoes, and Mexican crema, and season with salt and pepper. Cover, reduce the heat to low, and simmer, stirring occasionally, for 12 to 15 minutes. Remove from the heat.

4 Serve with *Arroz Mexicano* and *Refried Beans*.

TIP Add a touch of bright color by stirring in 1 cup canned golden corn kernels. Mexican crema is similar to crème fraîche in texture and flavor, and it has a mild, slightly sweet flavor, while sour cream is much thicker.

VEGETABLES

SPINACH-STUFFED JALAPEÑOS

YIELD: 4 TO 6 SERVINGS   PREP TIME: 15 MINUTES   COOK TIME: 15 MINUTES

Spinach-stuffed jalapeños are a fun and delicious treat perfect for any occasion. Removing the seeds and veins from the jalapeños and rinsing them with cold water before filling helps tame the heat of these spicy chiles. The filling, made with bacon, spinach, and cream cheese, is a tasty side dish all on its own. Serve with your favorite tacos or with an icy cold Michelada (page 190) to cheer on your favorite team.

Cooking spray
6 bacon slices, chopped
2 to 3 tablespoons chopped onion
1 garlic clove, finely minced
1½ (10-ounce) packages frozen spinach, thawed and drained
8 ounces cream cheese, softened
Salt
Freshly ground black pepper
10 to 12 fresh jalapeño peppers, halved lengthwise and seeded

1 Preheat the oven 350°F. Lightly grease a baking sheet with cooking spray.

2 In a medium nonstick skillet, fry the bacon over medium-high heat until cooked through. Drain all but 1 tablespoon of the bacon drippings.

3 Add the onion and sauté for 1 to 2 minutes, until it turns translucent. Add the garlic and sauté for an additional 30 seconds.

4 Stir in the spinach and cream cheese and mix until well combined. Season with salt and pepper. Remove from the heat and cool completely.

5 Fill each jalapeño pepper half with the spinach stuffing. Arrange the filled jalapeño halves on the prepared baking sheet. Bake for about 15 minutes.

TIP Remember to always wear plastic gloves when handling fresh chiles and to wash your hands with soap and baking powder immediately afterward.

ROASTED, SAUTÉED, GRILLED, OR BOILED

▽▽ ▽ ▽ ▽▽▽ ▽ ▽ ▽▽▽▽▽ ▽ ▽▽▽▽▽▽▽▽ ▽▽▽▽ ▽ ▽▽ ▽ ▽ ▽▽

There are so many ways you can prepare vegetables. Here are a few.

For quick and easy recipes like Champiñones con Rajas *(page 115) and* Espinacas con Queso *(page 119),* **sautéing**—*cooking in a lightly greased pan over high heat—is best. When sautéed, vegetables retain many of their vital vitamins and minerals, as well as their flavor and vibrant color. Sautéing is ideal for tender veggies like onions, chiles, and leafy greens.*

Roasting and grilling are my preferred cooking methods when preparing vegetables. Slowly roasting vegetables in the oven deepens their flavor and color and brings out their natural sweetness. My favorite veggies for roasting are sweet potatoes, carrots, pumpkin, calabacitas, potatoes, fresh chiles, and nopales. Veggies can be roasted whole wrapped in aluminum foil or cut up and baked on a baking sheet. To add more flavor to roasted veggies, toss with olive oil and a variety of herbs and spices like cumin, chile powder, oregano, rosemary, and thyme.

Grilling imbues the veggies with a rich, smoky flavor. Veggies can be grilled in much the same way as roasting: whole, wrapped in aluminum, and cut up directly on the grill for those beautiful cross-hatch marks. In the case of nopales, roasting or grilling eliminates most of the slimy liquid they naturally produce.

Boiling is a great way to speed up the cooking process of sautéing. Some veggies like potatoes, green beans, carrots, and chayotes benefit from parboiling. Also, the less time the vegetables are cooking in the oil or manteca, the less they absorb. Pay attention to how long the veggies spend in the boiling water. Different veggies soften at different rates; don't wait until they are a soggy mess—rather, pull them out when they are still slightly crisp, then rinse with cold water to prevent the residual heat from cooking the vegetables even more.

SEVEN

PICKLES, SALSAS & SAUCES

▽ ▽

Whoever said variety is the spice of life obviously never tried a Mexican salsa.

This chapter has the salsa or garnish to fit your taco needs. Throughout the next few pages, you'll learn to make traditional salsas like Chile de Molcajete *(roasted tomatillo and árbol chile salsa; page 132),* Salsa Taquera Roja *(spicy red taquería-style salsa; page 143), and* Pico de Gallo *(page 139).*

If it's salsa verde you prefer, we have several tasty presentations, including both Mild *and* Spicy Salsa Verde *(pages 145 and 146, respectively),* Avocado Salsa Verde *(page 144), and a no-cook version called* Salsa Cruda *(page 140).*

And because an authentic Mexican taco wouldn't be complete without a few classic garnishes, you'll also find recipes for Chiles Torreados *(page 135),* Cebollas Encurtidas *(page 131),* Jalapeños en Escabeche *(pickled jalapeño peppers; page 138), and my grandpa's famous* Chile de Rajas con Queso *(roasted peppers with cheese; page 134).*

Now you just have to decide which salsa or garnish to make to turn up the heat on dinner. And I'm sure busy cooks will appreciate that many of the recipes featured in this chapter can be made completely from scratch in 15 to 20 minutes.

PICKLES, SALSAS & SAUCES

CEBOLLAS ENCURTIDAS

YIELD: 1½ CUPS   PREP TIME: 3 HOURS 5 MINUTES

There are certain garnishes or toppings that are a must with a particular meal. For example, I can't imagine eating Cochinita Pibil *(page 52) or* tortas ahogadas *without a large pile of pickled red onions on top. The refreshing combination of sweet red onion, tart lime juice, and spicy serrano chiles also makes this side the perfect accompaniment for* Tacos de Barbacoa *(page 168) or* Carnitas *(page 45). The recipes will vary from family to family, and I think my family's is one of the easiest.*

1 large red onion,
  thinly sliced
2 serrano chiles, seeded and
  finely chopped
½ teaspoon coarse salt
Juice of 3 limes

1 In a large bowl, combine the onion and serrano chiles. Season with the salt. Pour the juice over and stir gently to combine.

2 Cover the bowl with plastic wrap and refrigerate for at least 3 hours before serving.

TIP *Kick up the heat by substituting a habanero pepper for the serranos.*

DAIRY FREE

VEG

CHILE DE MOLCAJETE

YIELD: 1½ CUPS   PREP TIME: 5 MINUTES   COOK TIME: 15 MINUTES

Yahualica—the small town my family calls home—is known for producing the best-tasting chile de árbol in the world, with an intense flavor, aroma, and spiciness. So, it's no wonder that chile de árbol is the key ingredient in my go-to salsa. This roasted tomatillo and árbol chile salsa is called chile de molcajete *because traditionally it is made in a molcajete, but it can also be made using a blender or food processor.*

25 dried chiles de árbol
1 garlic clove
1 pound tomatillos,
    husks removed
½ to 1 teaspoon coarse salt

1 Heat a comal, griddle, or nonstick skillet over medium-high heat. Roast the dried árbol chiles and the garlic, tossing occasionally, for about 1 minute. Remove from the comal and set aside. Reduce the heat to medium.

2 Roast the tomatillos on the comal over medium heat for 8 to 10 minutes, turning them occasionally, until the skin has started to char and the tomatillos have softened.

3 If using a molcajete, grind the roasted chiles de árbol in a molcajete with ½ teaspoon of coarse salt, until the chiles resemble red pepper flakes. Add the roasted tomatillos and garlic, lightly breaking up the tomatillos with the pestle while also mixing them in with the chile de árbol, until the mixture resembles a chunky salsa. Season with more salt, if necessary.

4 If using a blender or food processor, blend the roasted chiles de árbol, garlic, and half of the tomatillos in a blender until smooth. Add the remaining tomatillos and pulse for a few seconds until the salsa is the desired consistency. Transfer the salsa to a bowl and season with the salt.

TIP *Serve this fiery salsa over sunny-side up eggs for extra spicy* huevos rancheros.

CHILE DE RAJAS CON QUESO

YIELD: 4 TO 6 SERVINGS   PREP TIME: 10 MINUTES   COOK TIME: 20 MINUTES

Not only did I inherit my love of cooking from my abuelito, but I also inherited his obsession with roasted green chiles with queso, a platillo típico from the state of Chihuahua, made with roasted green chiles, onion, garlic, tomato, and lots of gooey melted queso Chihuahua. Like Pappy, I make this recipe using Anaheim chiles, but I add a couple of serranos for spice. It's great with grilled meats, but it also makes a delectable meatless filling for tacos.

8 Anaheim chiles
2 tablespoons vegetable oil
½ medium onion, sliced
2 garlic cloves, minced
2 serrano chiles, chopped
  (optional)
3 roma tomatoes, chopped
¾ teaspoon salt
2 cups shredded queso
  Chihuahua

1 Heat a comal, griddle, or nonstick skillet over medium-high heat. Roast the Anaheim chiles, turning occasionally, until charred all over. Transfer the roasted chiles to a plastic or paper bag and let sit for at least 5 minutes. Using your fingers or paper towels, peel off the charred skin. Remove the stems and seeds and cut the chiles into thin strips. Set aside.

2 In a large skillet, heat the oil over high heat. Add the onion and sauté for 2 to 3 minutes, stirring occasionally, until the onion is translucent. Add the garlic and serrano chiles (if using) and sauté for about 1 minute.

3 Stir in the roasted Anaheim chile strips, tomatoes, and salt. Cover, reduce the heat to low, and simmer, stirring occasionally, for 10 minutes. Remove from the heat.

4 Stir in the shredded cheese. Cover and let sit 5 minutes until the cheese has completely melted. Stir gently to combine.

TIP *For a spicier chile, try using poblano or Hatch chiles.*

CHILES TORREADOS

YIELD: 6 SERVINGS   PREP TIME: 5 MINUTES   COOK TIME: 10 MINUTES

Every evening, our local taquero sets up shop, fires up his plancha, and immediately starts to caramelize onions and toast green chiles in a little of the manteca he'll also use to fry meat. The tantalizing aromas travel through the air, announcing to the neighborhood that el taquero is open for business. No matter how long I've lived in the same neighborhood, I never tire of the sweet smell. Spoon the onions over your favorite tacos with two chiles torreados on the side.

1 tablespoon vegetable oil
12 serrano chiles
½ medium onion, sliced
1 garlic clove, minced
Juice of 1 lime
2 tablespoons Maggi Jugo
    Seasoning Sauce

1 In a medium skillet, heat the oil over medium-high heat. Add the serrano chiles and onion and sauté, turning occasionally, for 3 to 5 minutes, until the skin on the chiles starts to blister and char. Add the garlic, lime juice, and Maggi Jugo. Reduce the heat to low and cover.

2 Simmer the chiles, turning occasionally, until all of the liquid has evaporated and the chiles are cooked through, about 5 minutes.

TIP *Substitute fresh jalapeños or yellow chiles for the serranos.*

CREMA DE CHIPOTLE

YIELD: 1 CUP   PREP TIME: 5 MINUTES

Made with Mexican crema, chipotles in adobo, garlic, lime juice, and mayonnaise, this multipurpose sauce can be served atop batter-fried tacos de pescado and tacos de camarón and makes for a delicious dressing for salads or coleslaw, or even as a sauce for pastas. I've also poached fish and shrimp in this sauce. The possibilities truly are endless with this creamy chipotle wonder.

1 canned chipotle in adobo sauce
2 tablespoons canned chipotle adobo
½ cup Mexican crema or sour cream
½ cup mayonnaise
1 garlic clove, minced
Juice of 1 lime
¼ teaspoon ground cumin (optional)
Salt

Blend the chipotle and adobo sauce, chipotle adobo, crema, mayonnaise, garlic, and lime juice in a blender or food processor until smooth. Transfer to a serving bowl and season lightly with ground cumin (if using) and salt.

Brush this sauce over tilapia fillets. Broil in the oven for 10 to 12 minutes.

GUACAMOLE DE MOLCAJETE

YIELD: 1½ TO 2 CUPS   PREP TIME: 5 MINUTES

Sometimes the simplest recipes are the best tasting. Made with just three ingredients, you couldn't ask for an easier guacamole recipe. Impress your guests by preparing this simple guacamole in your molcajete just before serving. They won't believe how easy it is, and they'll soon be asking you to make more. This salsa is so easy even the kiddies can help; just make sure they don't touch the chiles.

2 serrano chiles, seeds and veins removed
½ to 1 teaspoon coarse salt, divided
3 ripe avocados, peeled and seeded

1 In a molcajete, grind the serrano chiles and ½ teaspoon of the salt until the salt dissolves completely. Add the avocados, one at a time, mashing them well after each addition. Season with more salt, if necessary.

2 If you don't have a molcajete, using a sharp knife, finely chop the serrano chiles. In a medium bowl, lightly mash the avocados with a potato masher or fork until creamy. Stir in the serrano chiles and season with the coarse salt.

 To prevent browning, cover freshly made guacamole with plastic wrap directly touching its surface.

JALAPEÑOS EN ESCABECHE

YIELD: 2 CUPS   PREP TIME: 10 MINUTES   COOK TIME: 10 MINUTES

Sure, the canned pickled jalapeños you buy at the supermarket are okay, but once you taste the fresh flavor of making them at home, you'll never go back to store-bought. Onion, carrots, and spices season the vinegar and jalapeños. The carrots take on some of the spicy flavor of the jalapeños (a tasty option for anyone in search of flavor but not heat). This goes great with Queso Fundido *(page 57),* Tacos Dorados *(page 178), or your favorite grilled meats.*

1 tablespoon vegetable oil

6 jalapeños, sliced

3 medium carrots, peeled and sliced

½ medium onion, sliced

1 garlic clove, minced

1 teaspoon coarse salt

½ teaspoon freshly ground black pepper

¼ teaspoon ground cumin

1 bay leaf

3 cilantro sprigs

¾ cup white vinegar

¾ cup water

1 Sterilize a jar, ring, and lid in boiling water. Using kitchen tongs, carefully remove the jar, ring, and lid from water to dry completely.

2 In a large skillet, heat the oil over medium-high heat. Add the jalapeños, carrots, and onion, and sauté, stirring occasionally, for 5 to 7 minutes, until the onion turns translucent. Remove from the heat.

3 Add the garlic, salt, pepper, cumin, and bay leaf to the jar and mix. Add the sautéed vegetables and cilantro. Pour in the vinegar. Top off with enough water to fill the jar, leaving a ¼-inch space at the top. Seal the jar, shaking contents gently to combine. Refrigerate for at least 24 hours before serving.

TIP *Have fun adding other vegetables like cauliflower and cooked nopales to the jalapeños.*

PICO DE GALLO

YIELD: 2 CUPS   PREP TIME: 5 MINUTES   COOK TIME: 30 MINUTES

Pico de Gallo, *also known as* salsa fresca *and* salsa mexicana, *is probably the most popular traditional Mexican salsa. Made with fresh ingredients in the colors of the Mexican flag, this classic salsa is quick and easy to prepare. For a fun twist, try mixing pico de gallo with chopped fresh mango, pineapple, grapefruit, orange, or tunas (prickly pears). Serve with* Carne Asada *(page 43), atop your favorite tacos, or with a big bowl of totopos.*

4 roma tomatoes, finely chopped

½ medium white onion, finely chopped

2 to 4 serrano chiles, seeded and finely chopped

1 teaspoon coarse salt

¼ to ½ cup finely chopped cilantro

In a large bowl, mix together the tomatoes, onion, and serrano chiles. Season with the salt. Cover and refrigerate for at least 30 minutes for the flavors to meld. Stir in the cilantro just before serving.

TIP Spoon 3 to 4 tablespoons of Pico de Gallo *into 1½ cups mashed avocado for a flavorful guacamole.*

SALSA CRUDA

YIELD: 1½ TO 2 CUPS   PREP TIME: 15 MINUTES

Salsa Cruda is a fresh, tangy salsa that you can whip up in just 15 minutes. There is no cooking whatsoever for this salsa. None. Nada! Salsa cruda is often served in Mexican restaurants as a dipping sauce for tortilla chips, but it's fresh flavor is delicious over seafood, grilled meats, or simply spread on a corn tortilla hot off the comal.

1 pound tomatillos, husks removed and cut into quarters

6 serrano chiles, stemmed and seeded

½ medium white onion, chopped

1 garlic clove

2 tablespoons chopped cilantro

Juice of 1 lime

½ cup water (optional)

¾ to 1 teaspoon coarse salt

Blend the tomatillos, serrano chiles, onion, garlic, cilantro, and lime juice in a blender until smooth. If the salsa is too thick, add the water, 1 tablespoon at a time, until the salsa reaches the desired consistency; it shouldn't be too thick or too watery. Season with the salt.

 For a spicier salsa, leave the chile seeds in.

SALSA DE CHILE GUAJILLO

YIELD: 2 CUPS   PREP TIME: 5 MINUTES   COOK TIME: 20 MINUTES

I love all dried chiles! From chiles de árbol to chiles ancho and chipotles, they each have unique flavor profiles all their own. But when it comes to the dried chile I use most in my cocina, guajillo chiles win hands down. I mainly use guajillos for the vibrant color they add to salsas and adobos, but in this recipe, the flavor of this underrated chile shines all on its own. Serve this salsa with grilled meats and seafood!

6 dried guajillo chiles
1½ cups water
½ medium white
  onion, chopped
1 garlic clove, minced
4 tomatoes
1 teaspoon coarse salt
½ teaspoon ground cumin
½ teaspoon ground
  Mexican oregano
¼ teaspoon freshly ground
  black pepper

1 Heat a comal, griddle, or nonstick skillet over high heat. Toast the dried chiles for 20 to 30 seconds per side. Transfer the chiles to a medium saucepan and add the water, onion, and garlic. Bring to a boil over high heat. Cover, reduce the heat to low, and simmer for 5 minutes, until the chiles have softened. Remove from the heat and cool slightly.

2 While the chiles are boiling, roast the tomatoes on the comal over medium-high heat, turning occasionally, until somewhat charred and softened.

3 Blend or process the tomatoes, guajillos and their cooking water, the onion, and the garlic in a blender or food processor until smooth. Transfer to a serving bowl and season with salt, cumin, oregano, and pepper.

 Stir this sauce into scrambled eggs for a delicious Mexican breakfast dish called chile de huevo *(eggs in chile sauce).*

SALSA DE TOMATE

YIELD: 4 TO 6 CUPS   PREP TIME: 5 MINUTES   COOK TIME: 20 MINUTES

I contemplated not adding this salsa recipe to the book, thinking it too simple, like the Mild Salsa Verde. But this salsa plays such an important role in so many Mexican dishes, I had to include it. Made with just-cooked ripe tomatoes and seasoned with red onion and Mexican oregano, this mild and delicious salsa is traditionally served over tostadas, burritos, and Tacos Dorados *(page 178). It can also be used to make* chilaquiles, entomatadas *(tomato sauce enchiladas), and even birria.*

2 pounds ripe roma
   tomatoes
¾ to 1 teaspoon coarse salt
½ medium red onion, thinly
   sliced (optional)
½ teaspoon dried oregano,
   crushed (optional)

1 In a large stockpot, place the tomatoes with enough water to cover. Bring to a boil over high heat. Cover, reduce the heat to low, and simmer for 15 to 20 minutes, until the tomatoes have softened. Remove from the heat and cool slightly.

2 Using a slotted spoon, carefully transfer the cooked tomatoes to a blender and blend until smooth. (Depending on the size of your blender, you may have to blend the cooked tomatoes in batches.)

3 Transfer the purée to a large bowl and season with the salt. If the sauce is too thick stir in 1 cup of the cooking water from the tomatoes. (The sauce should be about the same consistency as tomato sauce.) Stir in the red onion and oregano.

TIP   Replace the 1 cup of water used to thin the salsa with 1 cup of beef or chicken broth for a tasty caldillo de tomate *(tomato broth) to serve over* Tacos Dorados *(page 178), birria, tortas, and tostadas.*

SALSA TAQUERA ROJA

YIELD: 1½ TO 2 CUPS   PREP TIME: 5 MINUTES   COOK TIME: 20 MINUTES

Salsa Taquera Roja is similar to Chile de Molcajete *(page 132) in that the ingredients are identical: fresh tomatillos, dried chiles de árbol, and garlic. What makes this salsa unique is that the tomatillos and chiles are boiled first, resulting in a smoother salsa. Salsa taquera roja is often found alongside a mild salsa verde at most taquerías. Serve this tasty salsa over tacos and flautas or with a big bowl of chips at your next Mexican fiesta or football party.*

1 pound tomatillos,
  husks removed
3 cups water
20 dried árbol
  chiles, stemmed
1 garlic clove
½ teaspoon coarse salt

1 In a medium saucepan, bring the tomatillos and water to a boil over medium-high heat. Reduce the heat to low and simmer for 10 to 12 minutes, until tomatillos are cooked through. Remove from the heat.

2 Add the dried árbol chiles and soak for about 5 minutes, until the chiles have softened.

3 Using a slotted spoon, transfer the tomatillos and árbol chiles to a blender, add the garlic, and blend until smooth. Transfer the salsa to a serving bowl and season with the coarse salt.

TIP *Substitute 1 pound roma tomatoes for the tomatillos for an even more brightly hued salsa.*

PICKLES, SALSAS & SAUCES

AVOCADO SALSA VERDE

YIELD: 2 CUPS   PREP TIME: 5 MINUTES   COOK TIME: 15 MINUTES

Who can resist the creamy flavor of ripe avocados combined with a tangy spicy salsa verde? I know I can't! Whenever I make Salsa Verde Chicken Taquitos *(page 162), this salsa verde de aguacate (avocado green salsa) is a must! Not only is this a tasty dipping salsa for taquitos and tortilla chips, it's also delicious served over grilled chicken and baked salmon. Or you can substitute this salsa in your favorite enchilada recipe. (You can thank me later.)*

1 pound tomatillos, husks removed
2 serrano chiles
¼ medium onion
1 garlic clove
3 cups water
Handful cilantro leaves
2 ripe avocados, peeled and seeded
1 teaspoon coarse salt

1 In a medium saucepan, bring the tomatillos, serrano chiles, onion, garlic, and water to a boil over medium-high heat. Reduce the heat to low and simmer for 10 to 12 minutes, until the tomatillos are cooked through.

2 Using a slotted spoon, transfer the tomatillos, chiles, onion, and garlic to a blender. Add the cilantro and avocado and blend until smooth. Transfer the salsa to a serving bowl and season with the salt.

TIP   *Combine* Avocado Salsa Verde *with leftover rotisserie chicken for a quick and easy taco filling.*

MILD SALSA VERDE

YIELD: 1½ CUPS   PREP TIME: 5 MINUTES   COOK TIME: 15 MINUTES

Most taquerías offer a mild salsa verde to offset the spiciness of the Salsa Taquera Roja (page 143). Made just with fresh tomatillos, this salsa is a delicious option for anyone unaccustomed to eating super spicy foods. If you like heat, resist the temptation to add chiles, onion, or garlic to ratchet up this salsa. Trust me. Adding them defeats the purpose of making a simple mild salsa, and you would miss out on a quiet winner.

1 pound tomatillos,
   husks removed
3 cups water
½ teaspoon coarse salt

In a medium saucepan, bring the tomatillos and water to a boil over medium heat. Reduce the heat to low and simmer 10 to 12 minutes, until the tomatillos are cooked through. Remove from the heat and cool slightly. Using a slotted spoon, transfer the tomatillos to a blender and blend until smooth. Transfer to a serving bowl and season with coarse salt.

 Stir Mild Salsa Verde into your favorite soup for an added level of flavor.

DAIRY FREE

VEG

QUICK & EASY

SPICY SALSA VERDE

YIELD: 1 TO 1½ CUPS   PREP TIME: 5 MINUTES   COOK TIME: 15 MINUTES

This green salsa heated by serrano chiles and brightened by fresh cilantro is one of the first recipes my husband taught to me when we were newlyweds. Having married young (he was 22, and I had just turned 20), money was pretty tight during our first few months of marriage, but we always had this salsa in the refrigerator to flavor everything from simple quesadillas to refried beans. After 21 years (and counting) of wedded bliss, this salsa continues to be one of our favorites.

6 to 8 serrano chiles
¼ medium onion
1 garlic clove
1 pound tomatillos,
    husks removed
Handful of cilantro leaves
½ teaspoon coarse salt

1 Heat a comal, griddle, or nonstick skillet over medium-high heat. Roast the serrano chiles, onion, and garlic for 3 to 5 minutes, turning occasionally, until the chiles have softened and started to char. Remove from the comal and set aside.

2 Reduce the heat to medium. Roast the tomatillos on the comal for 8 to 10 minutes, turning occasionally, until the skin has started to char and the tomatillos have softened.

3 Blend the toasted serrano chiles, half of the tomatillos, the onion, and the garlic in a blender until smooth. Add the cilantro and the remaining tomatillos and blend until the salsa is the desired consistency. Pour the salsa into a serving bowl and season with the salt.

 For a milder salsa, decrease the number of serrano chiles to only 1 or 2 chiles.

RED VS GREEN SALSA

When it comes to deciding which salsa to serve with your tacos, there is an age-old question you must ask yourself: Do you prefer red or green salsa on your tacos? Because the two most popular types of salsas served at taquerías are salsa roja (red salsa) and salsa verde (green salsa). For some that might be an easy question to answer, while for others it's a little more complicated.

Before we get into how these two types of salsas differ (aside from the obvious difference in color), there is something important I must point out. A common misconception about salsas is that they're all fiery and spicy, which is completely untrue. The word salsa is Spanish for "sauce" and refers to any kind of sauce, whether it be spicy, mild, chunky, or smooth.

Tomatillos are the base ingredient in almost every salsa verde. Tomatillos are readily available in the produce section of the supermarket. They are easy to recognize by their thin husks. Salsa verde is prepared by either boiling or roasting the ingredients, or in the case of Salsa Cruda, the ingredients are left uncooked. Salsa verde can be made with a variety of fresh green chiles like jalapeños and serranos or roasted poblano peppers. Common additions to salsa verde include onion, garlic, and cilantro. And sometimes even lime juice, avocado, and Mexican crema are added.

Salsa roja is generally made with a tomato base. Like salsa verde, the ingredients for salsa roja are either boiled or roasted and can be made with many of the same ingredients including fresh green chiles. Dried chiles are also common ingredients used in salsa roja. The dried chiles add a touch of earthy smokiness to salsa roja that you won't find in salsa verde.

For some, choosing which kind of salsa to serve with their tacos is much like deciding which wine to serve with dinner. Like white wine, salsa verde pairs nicely with white meats like fish, chicken, and pork, while salsa roja—much like red wine—is enjoyed best when paired with red meats like beef, lamb, and goat.

Now, let me let you in on a little secret. You really can't go wrong no matter what kind of salsa you choose, because there are no set rules. All that really matters is that you have fun and enjoy your tacos.

EIGHT
TACOS, COMPOSED

▽ ▽ ▽ ▽ ▽ ▽ ▽ ▽ ▽ ▽ ▽ ▽ ▽ ▽ ▽ ▽ ▽ ▽ ▽ ▽ ▽ ▽ ▽ ▽

So far, we've covered all the steps that go into make mouthwatering tacos at home, from how to make tortillas from scratch to traditional Mexican taco fillings and guisados, and a delicious array of salsas. Now it's time to put it all together.

If it's classic Mexican tacos you're craving, we have Taquería-Style Tacos de Bistec *(page 176)*, Tacos de Carnitas *(page 169)*, Beer Batter–Fried Fish Tacos *(page 151)*, Tacos de Barbacoa *(page 168)*, Tacos al Pastor *(page 166)*, *and* Tacos de Chicharrón en Salsa Verde *(page 170)—just to name a few.*

If it's crunchy tacos you're craving, you want pick from Tacos Dorados de Papa *(page 174)*, Salsa Verde Chicken Taquitos *(page 162)*, Shredded Beef Taquitos Ahogadas *(page 161)*, Spicy Chipotle Tequila Shrimp Taquitos *(page 164)*, *and* Tex-Mex Ground Beef Tacos Dorados *(page 178)*.

We even have quite a few meatless options like Black Bean Taquitos *(page 152)*, Hibiscus Flower Tacos *(page 158)*, Taquitos de Queso Tricolor *(page 180)*, *and* Squash Blossom Tacos *(page 165)*.

Making authentic Mexican tacos at home is easy; the only difficult part will be choosing which recipe to make first.

TACOS, COMPOSED

BEER BATTER-FRIED FISH TACOS

YIELD: 4 TO 6 SERVINGS   PREP TIME: 10 MINUTES   COOK TIME: 15 MINUTES

It's been a couple of decades since I've traveled to Baja California, but the one memory I love from my many childhood trips is the delicious fish tacos enjoyed at our favorite roadside taquerías. Batter-fried fish showed up in the late '80s, when it became all the rage. When making fish tacos at home, I like to serve them on flour or whole-wheat tortillas with lots of fresh veggies, pico de gallo, and a creamy chipotle sauce.

6 *Beer Batter-Fried Tilapia* fillets (page 64)

12 soft taco-size flour tortillas

1½ cups shredded cabbage

1 cup shredded carrot

½ medium red onion, thinly sliced

2 avocados, peeled, pitted, and sliced

1½ cups *Pico de Gallo* (page 139)

1 cup *Crema de Chipotle* (page 136)

6 limes, cut into 4 wedges each

1 Roughly chop the fried fish fillets into bite-size pieces.

2 On a comal, griddle, or nonstick skillet, heat the flour tortillas over medium-high heat for 30 to 45 seconds, until soft and pliable. Transfer to a platter. Spoon about 3 tablespoons of fried fish down the center of each tortilla. Top each with a little of the cabbage, carrot, onion, avocado, and *Pico de Gallo*. Serve with *Crema de Chipotle* and lime wedges on the side.

TIP *Add a touch of vibrant color to these tacos by using red cabbage.*

BLACK BEAN TAQUITOS

YIELD: 6 TO 8 SERVINGS   PREP TIME: 5 MINUTES   COOK TIME: 40 MINUTES

Sometimes I get a craving for something crispy and fried, but don't want the hassle of preparing a meat filling. Black bean flautas are a meat-free filling perfect for any night of the week. Here, the sweetness of the caramelized onions in the filling enhances the flavor of the black beans.

2 tablespoons olive oil
1 tablespoon butter
1 medium onion, diced
3 cups black beans, drained
⅔ cup bean broth or water
½ teaspoon ground cumin
Salt
1 cup queso manchego, shredded
24 corn tortillas
1 to 1½ cups vegetable oil, for frying
Finely shredded lettuce
Mexican crema or sour cream
Chile de Molcajete (page 132)

TIP *Cut taquitos in half before frying to serve as appetizers for your next fiesta.*

1 In a medium skillet, heat the oil and butter over medium-high heat. Add the onion and sauté, stirring occasionally, for 2 to 3 minutes, until the onion turns translucent. Reduce the heat to low and continue to cook, stirring occasionally, for 15 minutes, or until the onion starts to caramelize.

2 Stir in the black beans, bean broth, and cumin, and season with salt. When the beans begin to boil, reduce the heat and lightly mash the black beans with a potato masher. Simmer the beans until they thicken slightly. Remove from the heat and stir in the cheese.

3 On a comal, griddle, or nonstick skillet, heat the corn tortillas over medium heat for 30 to 45 seconds, until soft and pliable. Transfer to a platter. Spoon 2 to 3 tablespoons of the black bean mixture down the center of each tortilla. Roll up the tortillas tightly, securing with a toothpick, if desired.

4 In a medium skillet, heat the oil over medium-high heat. Carefully add the taquitos and fry, about 6 at a time, for about 3 minutes per side, until crisp and golden brown. Transfer the fried taquitos to a paper towel–lined plate to drain any excess oil. Remove the toothpicks, if used, before serving.

5 To serve, garnish with shredded lettuce, Mexican crema, and *Chile de Molcajete*.

CAPRICHOS DE ADOBADA

YIELD: 4 TO 6 SERVINGS   PREP TIME: 10 MINUTES   COOK TIME: 25 MINUTES

A capricho is a delicious cross between a quesadilla and a Mexican street taco. The capricho base is a corn-tortilla quesadilla that is topped with your choice of traditional taquería meat fillings and garnishes. Caprichos are a great way to use up leftover taco fillings like chorizo, pork al pastor, arrachera, Cochinita Pibil *(page 52), or* Barbacoa de Res *(page 39). For garnishes, how about going the classic route with chopped onion and cilantro, or perhaps try* Cebollitas Asadas *(page 114) and* Ensalada de Nopales *(page 102)?*

1½ cups cooked pinto beans
24 corn tortillas
3 cups shredded
  Oaxaca cheese
Carne Adobada (page 42)
Chopped red onion,
  for garnish
Chopped cilantro,
  for garnish
Chile de Molcajete
  (page 132) or *Salsa
  Taquera Roja* (page 143)

1 In a small saucepan, heat the pinto beans over medium-high heat until heated through. Set aside.

2 On a comal, griddle, or nonstick skillet, heat the corn tortillas over medium-high heat for 30 to 45 seconds, until soft and pliable. Reduce the heat to medium. Sprinkle ¼ cup shredded Oaxaca cheese onto 12 of the tortillas and top with the remaining corn tortillas. Heat the quesadillas for about 1 minute per side, until the cheese has melted.

3 Spoon 2 to 3 tablespoons of *Carne Adobada* down the center of each quesadilla. Garnish with about 2 tablespoons of pinto beans, onion, cilantro, and your favorite salsa.

 Use flour tortillas instead of corn, and your capricho becomes another fun quesadilla taco known as a gringa.

TACOS, COMPOSED

CHICKEN TACOS DE MOLE

YIELD: 6 TO 8 SERVINGS   PREP TIME: 5 MINUTES   COOK TIME: 25 MINUTES

Ready-made mole paste is a godsend. I like to keep a couple of jars of mole paste in the pantry for when I need to get dinner on the table in a hurry. Just add a few shredded chicken breasts or leftover rotisserie chicken and dinner is served. Over the years, I've learned to make various mole sauces from scratch, but every once in a while I crave the mole that my grandparents made, which came directly from a jar.

2 tablespoons vegetable oil
½ medium onion, diced
2 garlic cloves, minced
1 (8.25-ounce) jar of
   mole paste
5 cups chicken
   broth, divided
¼ cup sugar
Salt
4 cups shredded
   chicken breast
18 to 24 corn tortillas
½ cup chopped onion,
   for garnish
½ cup chopped cilantro,
   for garnish
Arroz Mexicano (page 100)
Refried Beans (page 96)

1 In a large skillet, heat the oil over medium-high heat. Add the onion and sauté, stirring occasionally, for 2 to 3 minutes, until the onion turns translucent. Add the garlic and sauté for an additional 30 seconds. Reduce the heat to low.

2 Stir in the mole paste and 2 cups of the chicken broth, using a potato masher to help break up the mole paste until it's completely dissolved. Add the remaining chicken broth, sugar, and season with the salt. Stir in the shredded chicken and simmer until heated through. Remove from the heat.

3 On a comal, griddle, or nonstick skillet, heat the tortillas, for 30 to 45 seconds, until soft and pliable. Transfer to a platter. Spoon 2 to 3 heaping tablespoons of chicken mole down the center of each tortilla. Garnish with the chopped onion and cilantro. Serve with *Arroz Mexicano* and *Refried Beans*.

TIP *Don't throw away the glass mole jars! Remove the label and wash with soap and water for a cute juice glass.*

CHORIZO TACOS

YIELD: 6 TO 8 SERVINGS   PREP TIME: 5 MINUTES   COOK TIME: 15 MINUTES

My first visit to Mexico happened the summer before my fifth birthday. It was during that first of many summers I'd spend in Mexico that I tasted Mexican chorizo for the first time and learned to speak Spanish. Ever since then I've had a mild obsession with chorizo that moving to Mexico has only helped encourage.

1½ cups cooked pinto beans (*Frijoles de la Olla*, page 95)

½ cup bean broth or water

1 pound Mexican *Pork Chorizo* (homemade, page 56, or store-bought, casing removed)

24 corn tortillas

1½ cups finely chopped white onion

1½ cups finely chopped cilantro

Salsa Taquera Roja (page 143)

Mild Salsa Verde (page 145)

1 In a small saucepan, bring the pinto beans and bean broth to a boil over medium-high heat. Remove from the heat and set aside.

2 In a medium skillet, cook the chorizo over medium-high heat until lightly browned. Set aside.

3 On a comal, griddle, or nonstick skillet, heat the corn tortillas over medium-high heat for 30 to 45 seconds, until soft and pliable. Transfer to a platter. For each taco, stack 2 corn tortillas. Spoon 2 to 3 heaping tablespoons of cooked chorizo down the center of the top tortilla. Garnish with 2 tablespoons each of pinto beans, white onion, and cilantro. Serve with *Salsa Taquera Roja* and *Mild Salsa Verde*.

TIP *Pappy's famous* Chile de Rajas con Queso *(page 134) is a great all-in-one garnish for these tacos.*

FLAUTAS DE RAJAS

YIELD: 4 TO 6 SERVINGS   PREP TIME: 10 MINUTES   COOK TIME: 25 MINUTES

Traditionally, flautas and taquitos are fried in oil, but when I make them with flour tortillas, I prefer baking them in a hot oven until golden and crisp. Because these baked flautas are filled with roasted poblano pepper strips and requesón, they are a healthier menu option for a meatless dinner or light lunch.

Cooking spray
6 poblano peppers
1 tablespoon vegetable oil
½ medium onion,
   thinly sliced
Salt
12 flour tortillas
2 cups requesón or
   queso fresco
Mexican crema or
   sour cream
Avocado Salsa Verde
   (page 144)

> **TIP** *If you are unable to find poblano chiles, Anaheim or Hatch chiles can be used. Just increase the amount of chiles to 8 chiles as they are thinner than poblanos.*

1 Preheat the oven to 350°F. Lightly grease a baking sheet with cooking spray.

2 On a comal, griddle, or nonstick skillet, roast the poblano peppers over medium-high heat, turning occasionally, until the skin is charred all over. Place the peppers in a plastic or paper bag and let sit for at least 5 minutes. Using your fingers or paper towels, peel the charred skin from the peppers. Remove the stems and seeds and roughly chop the peppers.

3 In a large skillet, heat the oil over medium-high heat. Add the onion and chopped poblanos and sauté, stirring occasionally, for 4 to 5 minutes, until the onion turns translucent. Season with salt and remove from the heat.

4 On the comal, griddle, or nonstick skillet, heat the flour tortillas over medium-high heat for 30 to 45 seconds, until soft and pliable. Transfer to a platter. Spoon 2 to 3 tablespoons of requesón down the center of each tortilla. Top with a little of the roasted poblano–onion mixture. Tightly roll the tortillas like a taquito. Secure with a toothpick, if desired. Arrange the flautas seam-side down on the baking sheet. Bake for 15 minutes until golden and crisp. Remove the toothpicks before serving.

5 Serve with the crema, salsa, or your favorite salsa for dipping.

GRILLED ACHIOTE CHICKEN TACOS

YIELD: 4 TO 6 SERVINGS   PREP TIME: 3 HOURS 10 MINUTES   COOK TIME: 10 MINUTES

Whether you're grilling chicken cutlets for tacos or chicken legs for an easy laid-back afternoon with friends, one can never have too many grilled chicken recipes. My friends and family all agree that this tasty marinade made with orange juice, lime juice, and achiote paste estápa chuparse los dedos, which is Spanish for "is finger licking good!" Topped with a grilled pico de gallo salsa, these tacos are sure to become one of your grilling favorites.

1 (3.5-ounce) package achiote paste
1½ cups freshly squeezed orange juice
¼ cup freshly squeezed lime juice
3 garlic cloves, minced
½ teaspoon ground cumin
2 pounds chicken cutlets
Salt
12 to 18 corn tortillas
2 ripe avocados, peeled, pitted, and thinly sliced
½ cup chopped cilantro leaves
½ medium white onion, thinly sliced
Grilled pico de gallo (see tip)

1 Blend the achiote paste, orange juice, and lime juice in a blender until smooth. Transfer to a large glass bowl or 9x13-inch baking dish. Stir in the garlic and cumin. Add the chicken, mixing to coat. Season lightly with salt. Cover with plastic wrap, refrigerate, and marinate for at least 3 hours.

2 Preheat the grill over a medium flame and grill the chicken for 3 to 5 minutes per side. Remove from the heat and let rest for 5 minutes. Cut the chicken into thin strips or chop into bite-size pieces.

3 Heat the tortillas on the grill until soft and pliable. Transfer to a platter. Add the desired amount of grilled chicken to the tortillas and garnish with sliced avocado, cilantro leaves, and sliced onions. Top with grilled pico de gallo.

> *TIP* *To make grilled pico de gallo, grill 4 roma tomatoes, ½ medium white onion, and 2 serrano chiles until softened and lightly charred. Remove from the heat. Finely chop the tomatoes, onion, and chiles. Stir in 2 tablespoons finely chopped cilantro and season with salt.*

TACOS, COMPOSED

DAIRY FREE

VEG

HIBISCUS FLOWER TACOS

YIELD: 4 SERVINGS   PREP TIME: 15 MINUTES   COOK TIME: 20 MINUTES

Flor de Jamaica (dried hibiscus flowers) aren't just for making agua fresca. The rehydrated flowers are completely edible! My favorite ways to enjoy them are in quesadillas and tacos. The natural sweetness of the onion and the heat from the serrano chile enhance the tartness of the hibiscus flowers. If you have never tried them, this is the ideal recipe for experiencing their delicious flavor.

2 cups dried
    hibiscus flowers
4 cups water
2 tablespoons vegetable oil
1 medium onion, diced
1 serrano chile, seeded and
    finely chopped (optional)
1 garlic clove, minced
Salt
Freshly ground black pepper
12 corn tortillas
Chopped red onion,
    for garnish
Chopped cilantro,
    for garnish
Mild or *Spicy Salsa Verde*
    (pages 145 and 146,
    respectively)

1 In a medium saucepan, bring the hibiscus flowers and water to a boil over medium-high heat. Cover and remove from the heat. Let the flowers soak for 10 minutes. Using a slotted spoon, transfer the hibiscus flowers to a medium bowl and set aside.

2 In a large skillet, heat the oil over medium-high heat. Add the onion and serrano chile (if using) and sauté, stirring occasionally, for 2 to 3 minutes, until the onion turns translucent. Add the garlic and sauté for an additional 30 seconds. Stir in the hibiscus flowers, season with salt and pepper, and cook for 8 to 10 minutes, stirring occasionally.

3 On a comal, griddle, or nonstick skillet, heat the tortillas over medium-high heat for 30 to 45 seconds, until soft and pliable. Transfer to a platter. Spoon 2 to 3 heaping tablespoons of the hibiscus flower filling down the center of each tortilla. Garnish with the chopped red onion and cilantro. Top with the salsa.

TIP *Use the rehydration water from the hibiscus flowers to make* Agua de Jamaica *(page 188). You can find dried hibiscus flowers in the produce section or spice aisle of your supermarket, or you can order them online.*

LONGANIZA AND SWEET POTATO TACOS

YIELD: 4 TO 6 SERVINGS   PREP TIME: 10 MINUTES   COOK TIME: 30 MINUTES

Because sweet potatoes are mostly used to make sweet dishes like Camotes Enmielados *(page 113), I wanted to create something savory with authentic Mexican flavor, because I love using sweet potatoes in savory dishes. That is exactly how these tacos came to be.* Longaniza *(Mexican sausage) and sweet potato tacos are like a cross between* Papas con Chorizo *(page 121) and* Tacos al Pastor *(page 166).*

2 tablespoons vegetable oil
½ medium onion,
    coarsely chopped
1 garlic clove, minced
1 pound longaniza or chorizo
2 medium sweet potatoes,
    peeled and diced
¼ teaspoon ground cumin
¼ teaspoon paprika
Salt
Freshly ground black pepper
Juice of 1 orange
12 to 18 corn tortillas
Red onion, finely chopped,
    for garnish
Cilantro, finely chopped,
    for garnish

> TIP *The filling is also delicious in a burrito.*

1 In a large nonstick skillet, heat the oil over medium-high heat. Add the onion and sauté, stirring occasionally, for 2 to 3 minutes, until the onion turns translucent. Add the garlic and sauté for an additional 30 seconds. Add the longaniza and cook for 8 to 10 minutes, until lightly browned.

2 Add the sweet potatoes, cumin, and paprika, and season with salt and pepper. Squeeze the orange juice over the sweet potato and longaniza filling. Cover, reduce the heat to low, and simmer, stirring occasionally, until the sweet potatoes are tender and the orange juice has evaporated.

3 On a comal, griddle, or nonstick skillet, heat the corn tortillas over medium-high heat for 30 to 45 seconds, until soft and pliable. Transfer to a platter. Spoon 2 to 3 heaping tablespoons of the filling down the center of each tortilla. Garnish with the chopped red onion and cilantro. Serve with your favorite salsa.

PAN-FRIED FISH TACOS

YIELD: 4 TO 6 SERVINGS   PREP TIME: 10 MINUTES   COOK TIME: 15 MINUTES

Some of my fondest childhood memories are of fishing with my mom. By the time I was five years old, I had my own fishing pole and a cute little plastic tackle box. Mom and I spent hours sitting by the lake, waiting for the fish to bite. At the end of the day, my mom would fire up the grill or hot plate and cook our catch of the day. I haven't gone fishing in ages, but I still enjoy making mom's pan-fried fish with a light masa harina coating and serving it in tacos with lots of fresh veggies.

1 cup masa harina
1 teaspoon grated lime zest
1 teaspoon salt, plus more
    for seasoning
1 teaspoon paprika
½ teaspoon freshly ground
    black pepper, plus more
    for seasoning
1 cup milk
¼ cup vegetable oil,
    for frying
4 to 6 tilapia steaks,
    thawed, if frozen
12 soft tacos-sized whole-
    wheat tortillas
1½ cups shredded cabbage
1 cup shredded carrot
½ cup cilantro leaves
2 ripe avocados,
    thinly sliced
Lime wedges, for serving
Salsa Cruda (page 140)
    or *Crema de Chipotle*
    (page 136)

1 In a medium bowl, combine the masa harina, lime zest, salt, paprika, and pepper.

2 In a wide bowl, add the milk and season with salt and pepper.

3 Dip the tilapia fillets in seasoned milk, and then coat them with the masa harina mixture.

4 In a large nonstick skillet, heat the oil over medium-high heat. Fry the coated fillets for 3 to 5 minutes per side, until golden brown on the outside. Transfer the fillets to a paper towel–lined plate to drain any excess oil. Cut the fish into thin strips.

5 On a comal, griddle, or nonstick skillet, heat the tortillas over medium-high heat for 30 to 45 seconds, until soft and pliable. Transfer to a platter. Add a few strips of tilapia to each tortilla. Garnish the tacos with cabbage, carrot, cilantro, and avocado slices. Serve with lime wedges and *Salsa Cruda* or *Crema de Chipotle*.

TIP   These tacos can also be made with salmon fillets!

TAQUERÍA TACOS

SHREDDED BEEF TAQUITOS AHOGADAS

YIELD: 4 TO 6 SERVINGS   PREP TIME: 10 MINUTES   COOK TIME: 20 MINUTES

Like chicken taquitos, these beef taquitos made with leftover shredded beef are a delectable treat. Serving taquitos, tacos, burritos, or tortas ahogadas *means they are bathed in some kind of spicy sauce or salsa. Unlike burritos and tortas ahogadas that soften with the sauce, taquitos maintain their crunch. Serve with* Salsa de Chile Guajillo *(page 141), whose deep red color; sweet, earthy flavor; and mild heat are the perfect counterpoint.*

⅓ cup *Salsa de Chile Guajillo* (page 141)

12 corn tortillas

3 cups shredded beef (such as *Asado de Res a la Cerveza*, page 38)

1 cup vegetable oil, for frying

Shredded cabbage, for garnish

Chopped white onion, for garnish

1 cup crumbled queso fresco

> **TIP** *Have fun making* Tacos Ahogados *with different salsas, like* Chile de Molcajete *(page 132),* Spicy Salsa Verde *(page 146), and* Avocado Salsa Verde *(page 144).*

1 In a small saucepan, heat the salsa over medium heat. Set aside.

2 On a comal, griddle, or nonstick skillet, heat the tortillas over medium-high heat for 30 to 45 seconds, until soft and pliable. Transfer to a platter. Spoon 3 heaping tablespoons of the shredded beef close to the edge of each tortilla. Roll the tortillas tightly to form taquitos and secure with toothpicks, if desired.

3 In a medium nonstick skillet, heat the oil over medium-high heat. Fry the taquitos, four to six at a time, for about 3 minutes per side, until golden and crisp. Transfer the taquitos to a paper towel–lined plate to drain any excess oil.

4 Serve two or three taquitos on each plate. Ladle the guajillo salsa over the taquitos. Garnish with shredded cabbage, chopped white onion, and crumbled queso fresco.

SALSA VERDE CHICKEN TAQUITOS

YIELD: 4 TO 6 SERVINGS   PREP TIME: 15 MINUTES   COOK TIME: 20 MINUTES

Down the street from where my grandparents lived was a small family-owned, fast-food Mexican restaurant that specialized in tacos and burritos. My favorite dish on the menu was the chicken taquitos with extra guacamole. It was the only thing I ever ordered, not because I was a picky eater, but because chicken taquitos are just that good. Adding a little salsa verde *(see chapter 7) to the shredded chicken adds a level of flavor that pairs well with guacamole.*

4 cups shredded
  cooked chicken
½ medium onion,
  finely chopped
1 garlic clove, minced
Salt
Freshly ground black pepper
2 cups *Avocado Salsa Verde*,
  (page 144) divided
1 cup Mexican crema or
  sour cream, divided
1 cup shredded
  Chihuahua cheese
12 to 18 corn tortillas
1½ cups vegetable oil,
  for frying
Shredded lettuce
1 cup crumbled queso cotija
Frijoles Borrachos (page 101)
Arroz Mexicano (page 100)

1 In a large bowl, combine the chicken, onion, and garlic. Season lightly with salt and pepper. Add ¾ cup of the salsa, ¼ cup of the crema, and the cheese and mix well.

2 On a comal, griddle, or nonstick skillet, heat the tortillas over medium-high heat for 30 to 45 seconds, until soft and pliable. Transfer to a platter. Spoon 2 to 3 tablespoons of the chicken mixture close to the edge of each tortilla. Tightly roll into taquitos and secure with a toothpick, if desired.

3 In a large skillet, heat the oil over medium-high heat. Fry the taquitos, six to eight at a time, for about 3 minutes per side, until golden and crisp. Transfer the taquitos to a paper towel–lined plate to drain any excess oil. Season the taquitos lightly with salt, if desired. Remove the toothpicks before serving.

4 Serve 3 or 4 taquitos on each plate. Top with shredded lettuce and a sprinkling of crumbled queso cotija. Drizzle the remaining ¾ cup of the crema and the remaining 1¼ cups of the salsa on top. Serve with *Frijoles Borrachos* and *Arroz Mexicano*.

TIP *Avoid the hassle of frying by baking the taquitos on a lightly greased baking sheet at 400°F for 15 to 18 minutes.*

SPICY CHIPOTLE TEQUILA SHRIMP TAQUITOS

YIELD: 4 SERVINGS   PREP TIME: 5 MINUTES   COOK TIME: 30 MINUTES

Don't you love those recipes that taste like you spent a lot of time in the kitchen, but in reality take only 30 minutes to prepare? That is just one of many reasons I love these spicy shrimp tacos flavored with canned chipotles, fresh lime juice, and tequila (because I'm always looking for an excuse to add tequila to recipes). The lingering flavor of the chipotle and tequila is a delight for your taste buds.

1 tablespoon extra-virgin olive oil

1 tablespoon butter

1 pound medium shrimp, peeled, deveined, and roughly chopped

¼ cup tequila

2 tablespoons freshly squeezed lime juice

2 canned chipotles in adobo, finely chopped

12 corn tortillas

½ cup vegetable oil

1 cup shredded cabbage

½ cup cilantro leaves

Lime wedges, for garnish

Crema de Chipotle (page 136)

> **TIP** *If canned chipotles are too spicy for your taste, try adding a couple of tablespoons of just the adobo sauce for an intense smoky flavor without the heat.*

1 In a medium skillet, heat the olive oil and butter over medium-high heat until the butter has melted. Add the shrimp and sauté for 3 to 5 minutes, until bright orange.

2 Stir in the tequila, lime juice, and chipotles. Cover and simmer for about 5 minutes or until all of the liquid has evaporated. Remove from the heat.

3 On a comal, griddle, or nonstick skillet, heat the corn tortillas over medium-high heat for 30 to 45 seconds, until soft and pliable. Transfer to a platter. Spoon 2 to 3 tablespoons of the shrimp filling close to the edge of each tortilla. Roll the tortillas tightly to form taquitos and secure with toothpicks, if desired.

4 In a medium nonstick skillet, heat the vegetable oil over medium-high heat. Fry the taquitos, 4 at a time, for about 3 minutes per side, until golden and crisp. Transfer the taquitos to a paper towel–lined plate to drain any excess oil.

5 Serve 2 or 3 taquitos on each plate. Garnish with shredded cabbage, cilantro leaves, and lime wedges. Serve with *Crema de Chipotle.*

SQUASH BLOSSOM TACOS

YIELD: 4 SERVINGS   PREP TIME: 5 MINUTES   COOK TIME: 15 MINUTES

When squash blossoms are in bloom, I cannot get enough of them. You've probably already tried or at least heard about adding them to salads, quesadillas, and soups or stuffing them with cheese and frying them in a light, airy batter. But flores de cala-baza *can also be sautéed a la Mexicana with onion, tomatoes, and chiles for a simple filling for tacos and quesadillas.*

1 pound squash blossoms, stemmed and stamens removed

2 tablespoons olive oil

½ medium onion, finely chopped

1 to 2 serrano chiles, seeded and finely chopped

2 medium tomatoes, seeded and finely chopped

Salt

12 corn tortillas

1 cup crumbled queso fresco

Chile de Molcajete (page 132), Mexican crema, or guacamole

1 Rinse the squash blossoms with cold water and pat dry with paper towels. Roughly chop the squash blossoms.

2 In a medium skillet, heat the oil over medium-high heat. Add the onion and chiles and sauté, stirring occasionally, for 2 to 3 minutes, until the onion turns translucent. Add the tomatoes and sauté for an additional 2 to 3 minutes. Season with salt. Stir in the squash blossoms and sauté just until they start to wilt. Remove from the heat.

3 On a comal, griddle, or nonstick skillet, heat the tortillas over medium-high heat for 30 to 45 seconds, until soft and pliable. Transfer to a platter. Spoon about 3 tablespoons of the filling down the center of the tortillas. Top with the queso fresco. Serve with *Chile de Molcajete*, Mexican crema, or guacamole.

 If squash blossoms aren't in season, you can also substitute roughly chopped spinach or kale.

DAIRY FREE

TACOS AL PASTOR

YIELD: 6 TO 8 SERVINGS   PREP TIME: 3 HOURS 15 MINUTES   COOK TIME: 60 MINUTES

Tacos al Pastor *are one of the most popular tacos Mexico has to offer. Thin slices of pork meat marinated in a chile and herb adobo are stacked high on a trompo and topped with a whole pineapple (peeled) and onion, then slow roasted for hours until juicy and tender. But because most of us don't have a spit, I have a great recipe for making these tacos at home. The hardest part in making these tacos is waiting the three hours for the meat to marinate.*

3 dried ancho chiles, stemmed and seeded

2 dried guajillo chiles, stemmed and seeded

2 cups water

2 chipotles in adobo sauce

2 garlic cloves

½ medium onion

¼ cup white vinegar

1½ teaspoons coarse salt

1 teaspoon ground cumin

½ teaspoon freshly ground black pepper

½ teaspoon dried oregano

2 pounds pork shoulder roast, finely chopped

2 tablespoons manteca de cerdo, bacon grease, or vegetable oil

1½ cups diced fresh pineapple

1 cup orange juice

18 to 24 corn tortillas

1 cup chopped white onion

½ cup chopped cilantro

Lime wedges, for garnish

Chile de Molcajete (page 132)

Chiles Torreados (page 135)

1 In a medium saucepan, bring the dried chiles and water to a boil over high heat. Cover, reduce the heat to low, and simmer for about 5 minutes, until the chiles have softened. Remove from the heat and let cool to room temperature.

2 Blend the chiles, their cooking water, the chipotles in adobo, garlic, onion, vinegar, salt, cumin, pepper, and oregano in a blender until smooth.

3 In a large bowl or baking dish, combine the chopped pork and the chile sauce, mixing until the meat is completely coated. Cover with plastic wrap and refrigerate for at least 3 hours and up to overnight.

4 To cook, in a large skillet, heat the manteca over high heat. Add the pork and cook, stirring occasionally, for 5 to 7 minutes, until cooked through. Stir in the fresh pineapple and orange juice. Cover, reduce the heat to low, and simmer, stirring occasionally, for 40 to 45 minutes, until all of the juices from the meat and adobo sauce have evaporated and the meat has started to brown.

5 On a comal, griddle, or nonstick skillet, heat the tortillas over medium-high heat for 30 to 45 seconds, until soft and pliable. Transfer to a platter. Spoon 2 to 3 heaping table-spoons of the filling down the center of each tortilla. Garnish with chopped white onion, cilantro, and lime wedges. Serve with *Chile de Molcajete* and *Chiles Torreados*.

TIP *Serve al pastor filling on warm pita bread or whole-wheat tortillas for tacos Árabes.*

TACOS DE BARBACOA

YIELD: 4 TO 6 SERVINGS   PREP TIME: 10 MINUTES   COOK TIME: 15 MINUTES

Made with Barbacoa de Res *(page 39),* Tacos de Barbacoa *can be served one of two ways. The simplest way is serving chopped barbacoa beef on warm flour tortillas with chopped white onion and cilantro and using the chile broth as the salsa. But my favorite way is dipping a meat-filled taco in the chile broth, then frying it in hot oil until almost crisp. These tacos are so good, all you need for garnish are some* Cebollas Encurtidas *(page 131) and* Chiles Torreados *(page 135).*

12 corn tortillas
2 ½ to 3 cups shredded
   Barbacoa de Res (page 39)
¼ to ½ cup vegetable oil,
   for frying
1 cup chile broth from
   Barbacoa de Res (page 39)
Cebollas Encurtidas
   (page 131)
Lime wedges, for serving
Chiles Torreados (page 135,
   optional)

1 On a comal, griddle, or nonstick skillet, heat the tortillas over medium-high heat for 30 to 45 seconds, until soft and pliable. Transfer to a platter. Spoon 2 to 3 heaping tablespoons of barbacoa beef down the center of each tortilla. Fold the tortillas in half.

2 In a large nonstick skillet, heat the oil over medium-high heat. Dip the tacos in the chile broth. Carefully add the tacos to the skillet and fry, about 5 minutes per side, until slightly crispy. Transfer the fried tacos to a paper towel–lined plate to drain any excess oil.

3 Place two or three tacos on each plate. Top with *Cebollas Encurtidas*. Serve with lime wedges and *Chiles Torreados*, if desired.

For a complete meal, serve these tacos with Frijoles Adobados *(page 98),* Poblano Rice *(page 105), and* Horchata de Avena *(page 187).*

TACOS DE CARNITAS

YIELD: 4 TO 6 SERVINGS PREP TIME: 10 MINUTES COOK TIME: 20 MINUTES

When hosting a party or entertaining guests, more often than not we are serving pork Carnitas (page 45). It's a no-fuss meal that everyone loves. And because I always make enough to feed a small army, I always have leftovers. But I'm not complaining! Tacos de Carnitas are an easy and delicious way to use up our leftover carnitas. Keep the garnishes simple with just queso fresco, sliced avocado, red onion, and cilantro. And serve with Pico de Gallo (page 139) and Guacamole de Molcajete (page 137).

3 cups shredded pork
  Carnitas (homemade,
  page 45, or store-bought)
12 corn tortillas
1 cup crumbled queso fresco
2 ripe avocados, peeled,
  seeded, and sliced
½ cup chopped cilantro
½ cup chopped red onion
Lime wedges, for serving
Frijoles Borrachos (page 101)
Pico de Gallo (page 139)
Guacamole de Molcajete
  (page 137)

1 In a large nonstick skillet, reheat the carnitas over medium-high heat.

2 On a comal, griddle, or nonstick skillet, heat the tortillas over medium-high heat for 30 to 45 seconds, until soft and pliable. Transfer to a platter. Spoon 3 to 4 generous tablespoons of shredded carnitas down the center of each tortilla. Garnish with crumbled queso fresco, 1 or 2 slices of avocado, chopped cilantro, and chopped onion. Serve with lime wedges, *Frijoles Borrachos*, *Pico de Gallo*, and *Guacamole de Molcajete*.

TIP *Add the juice of 1 orange to the pork carnitas when reheating. Simmer until all of the juice has evaporated and the carnitas start to caramelize. Orange juice or cola-flavored soda are added to traditionally prepared carnitas because the sugar in the liquids helps caramelize the carnitas, making them crisp on the outside and juicy on the inside.*

TACOS DE CHICHARRÓN EN SALSA VERDE

YIELD: 4 TO 6 SERVINGS   PREP TIME: 5 MINUTES   COOK TIME: 20 MINUTES

If you like bacon, you have to try chicharrónes. Not to be confused with the pork rinds you find in the chip aisle, chicharrónes are crispy fried pieces of meaty pork skin. Chicharrónes are so good just on their own, all you really need is a stack of warm corn tortillas and your favorite Mexican salsa. But simmering the chicharrónes in Spicy Salsa Verde *softens them ever so slightly, making them even better.*

1 pound pressed
   chicharrónes, cut into
   bite-size pieces
2 cups *Spicy Salsa Verde*
   (page 146)
24 corn tortillas

1 In a large nonstick skillet, heat the chicharrónes over low heat. Let the chicharrónes cook slowly in their own fat, stirring occasionally, for 8 to 10 minutes, or until lightly browned. Stir in the salsa and simmer, for 8 to 10 minutes, until the salsa starts to boil. Remove from the heat.

2 On a comal, griddle, or nonstick skillet, heat the corn tortillas over medium-high heat for 30 to 45 seconds, until soft and pliable. For each taco, stack 2 corn tortillas on top of each other. Spoon 2 to 3 tablespoons of chicharrón en salsa verde down the center of each top tortilla.

TIP *Look for pressed chicharrónes at your local Latin super-market. Note that there really isn't a good substitution for chicharrónes. If you'd like to make a slightly different recipe, try using pork rinds, but the texture will be much softer. Add 1 tablespoon of vegetable oil to the skillet and decrease the cooking time to 2 to 3 minutes.*

TAQUERÍA TACOS

TACOS DE LONGANIZA CON PIÑA

YIELD: 4 SERVINGS   PREP TIME: 5 MINUTES   COOK TIME: 25 MINUTES

I love Tacos al Pastor (page 166), but I don't always have time to prepare the marinade and marinate the meat overnight. That is a recipe I save for the weekends, when I have more time to spend in la cocina. But for those occasions when I'm craving tacos al pastor during the week, these tacos made with Mexican longaniza sausage and crushed pineapple are a quick and easy alternative that taste just like Tacos al Pastor. Sometimes my husband can't even tell the difference.

2 tablespoons vegetable oil

1 pound Mexican longaniza sausage, casing removed

Salt, optional

1 (14-ounce) can pineapple chunks and their juice

¼ teaspoon ground cumin

8 to 12 corn tortillas

½ cup chopped red onion

½ cup chopped cilantro

Salsa Taquera Roja (page 143)

Mild Salsa Verde (page 145)

1 In a medium skillet, heat the oil over medium-high heat. Add the longaniza and cook, lightly mashing with a spatula or wooden spoon to break up the sausage, for 8 to 10 minutes, until cooked through. Season lightly with salt (if using). Add the pineapple chunks and their juice and cumin. Cover and bring to a boil, reduce the heat to low, and simmer, stirring occasionally, for 12 to 15 minutes, until the juices have evaporated completely.

2 On a comal, griddle, or nonstick skillet, heat the tortillas over medium-high heat for 30 to 45 seconds, until soft and pliable. Spoon 2 to 3 heaping tablespoons of filling down the center of each tortilla. Garnish with the chopped red onion and cilantro. Serve with *Salsa Taquera Roja* or *Mild Salsa Verde*.

TIP   If you are unable to find longaniza, use Mexican chorizo.

TACOS DE POLLO A LA MEXICANA

YIELD: 4 TO 6 SERVINGS   PREP TIME: 10 MINUTES   COOK TIME: 25 MINUTES

Chicken tacos are the only kind of tacos that aren't sold at any of the taquerías in town. I have no idea why tacos de pollo aren't more popular in our small town, but thankfully they're easy to make at home. Gramm always added extra chicken to her chicken soup just so she could make tacos de pollo a la Mexicana with chopped tomato, onion, and bell pepper. I still prepare Gramm's chicken tacos, but I add a couple of serrano chiles for heat.

2 tablespoons vegetable oil
1 green bell pepper, chopped
½ medium onion, diced
1 or 2 serrano chiles, stemmed and seeded, finely chopped
2 garlic cloves, minced
4 cups shredded cooked chicken
3 roma tomatoes, diced
1 cup chicken broth
½ cup finely chopped cilantro, divided
½ teaspoon ground cumin
Salt
12 to 18 corn tortillas
3 ripe avocados, peeled and diced
Lime wedges, for garnish
Mexican crema or sour cream, for garnish

1 In a large skillet, heat the oil over high heat. Add the bell pepper, onion, and serrano chile, and sauté, stirring occasionally, for 3 to 5 minutes, until the onion turns translucent. Add the garlic and sauté for an additional 30 seconds. Stir in the shredded chicken, tomatoes, broth, ¼ cup of the chopped cilantro, cumin, and salt. Cover, reduce the heat to low, and simmer, stirring occasionally, for 12 to 15 minutes.

2 On a comal, griddle, or nonstick skillet, heat the tortillas over medium-high heat for 30 to 45 seconds, until soft and pliable. Spoon 2 to 3 heaping tablespoons of chicken down the center of each tortilla. Garnish with the remaining ¼ cup of the cilantro and the avocado. Serve with lime wedges and Mexican crema or sour cream.

TIP *This is a great recipe to use up leftover rotisserie chicken or Thanksgiving turkey.*

TACOS DE POLLO A LA PLANCHA

YIELD: 4 SERVINGS   PREP TIME: 5 MINUTES   COOK TIME: 15 MINUTES

The chicken cutlets seasoned with ancho chile powder, ground cumin, and oregano in this recipe cook up in no time at all on the stove top, making this a great weeknight dinner. You'll devour them topped with Salsa Cruda *(page 140),* Salsa Taquera Roja *(page 143), Mexican crema, or* Guacamole de Molcajete *(page 137). (If you're firing up the grill, make* Tacos de Pollo Asado *instead.)*

2 tablespoons ancho
   chile powder
½ teaspoon ground cumin
¼ teaspoon
   crushed oregano
1 pound chicken cutlets
Salt
Freshly ground black pepper
2 tablespoons olive oil
8 soft taco-size flour
   tortillas
1½ cups shredded
   red cabbage
½ cup finely chopped
   cilantro leaves
½ medium red onion,
   thinly sliced
Lime wedges, for garnish
Mexican crema or
   guacamole, for serving

1 In a small bowl, mix together the chile powder, cumin, and oregano. Sprinkle both sides of the chicken cutlets with salt and pepper, then with the chile powder mixture.

2 In a large nonstick skillet, heat the oil over medium-high heat. Add the seasoned chicken cutlets, cover the skillet, and cook for 5 to 7 minutes per side until cooked through. Cut the chicken cutlets into thin strips.

3 On a comal, griddle, or nonstick skillet, heat the tortillas over medium-high heat for 30 to 45 seconds, until soft and pliable. Transfer to a platter. Divide the chicken strips among the tortillas. Garnish with a handful of fresh red cabbage, cilantro leaves, sliced red onion, and lime wedges. Serve with Mexican crema or guacamole.

TIP *Substitute turkey cutlets for the chicken.*

TACOS, COMPOSED

173

TACOS DORADOS DE PAPA

YIELD: 6 SERVINGS   PREP TIME: 5 MINUTES   COOK TIME: 30 MINUTES

My husband introduced me to these tacos shortly after we married, and they are still one of his all-time favorite meals. Topped with shredded cabbage, crumbled queso cotija, and a mild tomato salsa, these tacos are a delicious meatless meal. Serve with Jalapeños en Escabeche *(page 138) or* Chiles Torreados *(page 135) for a spicy kick.*

4 medium potatoes, peeled and cut into quarters

4 cups water

Salt

Freshly ground black pepper

18 corn tortillas

1 cup plus 2 tablespoons asadero cheese, shredded, or Monterey Jack or provolone cheeses, shredded

1 to 1½ cups vegetable oil, for frying

Shredded cabbage or lettuce, for garnish

Mild *Salsa de Tomate* (page 142)

Crumbled queso cotija or queso fresco, for garnish

Jalapeños en Escabeche (page 138) or your favorite bottled hot sauce, for serving

TIP *This is a great recipe to use up leftover mashed potatoes.*

1 In a medium saucepan, bring the potatoes and water to a boil over medium-high heat. Cover, reduce the heat to low, and simmer for 10 to 12 minutes until tender. Drain. Season the potatoes with salt and pepper. Mash them lightly with a fork or potato masher.

2 On a comal, griddle, or nonstick skillet, heat the tortillas over medium-high heat for 30 to 45 seconds, until soft and pliable. Transfer to a platter. Spoon 2 to 3 tablespoons of the mashed potatoes down the center of each tortilla. Top with 1 tablespoon of shredded asadero cheese. Fold the tortillas in half, forming a taco.

3 In a large skillet, heat the oil over medium-high heat. Carefully fry the tacos, three or four at a time, for about 3 minutes per side, until golden and crisp on both sides. Transfer the tacos to a paper towel–lined plate to drain any excess oil.

4 To serve, place three tacos on each plate. Garnish with shredded cabbage. Spoon about ⅓ cup of mild *Salsa de Tomate* over the tacos. Sprinkle a little queso cotija on top. Serve with *Jalapeños en Escabeche* or your favorite bottled hot sauce.

TACOS DE COCHINITA PIBIL

YIELD: 4 TO 6 SERVINGS   PREP TIME: 10 MINUTES   COOK TIME: 15 MINUTES

Tacos are a great way to use leftovers, especially when it comes to exquisite traditional Mexican dishes like Cochinita Pibil *(page 52). So easy to put together with just corn tortillas topped with fresh cilantro and pickled red onions, these tacos are so delicious, no one will ever guess you're serving leftovers. This is one of the few tacos with which I don't serve salsa or guacamole, because I prefer to let the flavor of the achiote paste and spices in the* Cochinita Pibil *shine through. Serve with* Frijoles Adobados *(page 98) on the side.*

3 cups shredded *Cochinita Pibil* (page 52)
24 corn tortillas
Cebollas Encurtidas (page 131)
¾ cup chopped cilantro leaves (optional)
Lime wedges, for serving

1 In a medium skillet, reheat the *Cochinita Pibil* over medium-high heat for 12 to 15 minutes, until heated through.

2 On a comal, griddle, or nonstick skillet, heat the tortillas over medium-high heat for 30 to 45 seconds, until soft and pliable. Transfer to a platter. For each taco, stack 2 corn tortillas on top of each other. Spoon 3 to 4 tablespoons of the *Cochinita Pibil* down the center of the top tortilla. Top each with the *Cebollas Encurtidas* and cilantro leaves (if using). Serve with lime wedges.

TIP *For a festive presentation, serve the cooked* Cochinita Pibil *atop a banana leaf–lined platter.*

TACOS, COMPOSED

TAQUERÍA-STYLE TACOS DE BISTEC

YIELD: 4 TO 6 SERVINGS   PREP TIME: 15 MINUTES   COOK TIME: 30 MINUTES

I love tacos de bistec for a few reasons. One, the meat filling is super easy to prepare—brown the meat and season with salt and pepper. And two, thin-cut steak is often on sale, which makes this recipe budget-friendly. But the main reason is because tacos de bistec were my go-to tacos as a child.

Believe it or not, I wasn't always the adventurous foodie I am today. Whenever I traveled to Mexico with my grandparents, I was always afraid I'd end up eating some exotic meat like sesos (beef brains) or riñones (kidneys) that Pappy loved and couldn't wait to devour once we crossed the border (at five years old, can you really blame me?). And because not all taquerías offer chicken or fish, I quickly learned that tacos de bistec were my safest bet. And it didn't hurt that the browned-to-perfection pieces of thin-cut steak were mouthwatering and delicious.

Make these tacos extra special by recreating the taquería experience at home—it's great fun for the entire family and easy to do. Offer traditional garnishes like cooked beans, chopped white onion and cilantro, lime wedges, thinly sliced radishes, and a variety of mild and spicy salsas (homemade or store-bought).

2 tablespoons vegetable oil

2 pounds thin-cut sirloin steak, roughly chopped

Salt

Freshly ground black pepper

2 cups cooked pinto beans

1 to 1½ cups bean broth (from bean cooking water or canned)

1 tablespoon manteca, divided

36 corn tortillas

½ medium onion, finely chopped

½ cup finely chopped cilantro

1 cup thinly sliced radishes

Salsa Taquera Roja (page 143)

Mild Salsa Verde (page 145)

Lime wedges, for serving

Chiles Torreados (page 135)

1 In a large skillet, heat the oil over medium-high heat. Add the sirloin steak and sauté for 12 to 15 minutes, until no longer pink. Season with salt and pepper. Cover, reduce the heat to low, and simmer, stirring occasionally, for 15 to 20 minutes, until all the juices have evaporated. Uncover the skillet and increase the heat to high. Continue to cook, stirring often, for 8 to 10 minutes, until lightly browned. Remove from the heat.

2 While the meat is cooking, in a small saucepan, heat the pinto beans and the broth over medium-high heat.

3 Heat a comal, griddle, or nonstick skillet over medium-high heat. Melt about ½ teaspoon of the manteca on the comal for each batch of the tortillas. Heat the corn tortillas, four to six at a time, for 30 to 45 seconds, until soft and pliable. Transfer to a platter. For each taco, stack 2 corn tortillas on top of each other. Spoon 2 to 3 tablespoons of bistec down the center of top tortilla. Garnish the tacos with the cooked pinto beans, onion, cilantro, and radishes. Serve with the salsas, lime wedges, and Chiles Torreados.

TIP *You can also make these tacos with* Carne Adobada *(page 42) or* Asado de Res a la Cerveza *(page 38).*

TACOS, COMPOSED

177

TEX-MEX GROUND BEEF TACOS DORADOS

YIELD: 4 TO 6 SERVINGS   PREP TIME: 10 MINUTES   COOK TIME: 50 MINUTES

Hard to believe, but the ground beef taco filling that is ever so popular north of the border isn't even a thing down here in Mexico. You can take the girl out of the USA, but you can't take away her love for Americanized Mexican food. And even though I'm surrounded by authentic Mexican food, I still sometimes crave those ground beef crunchy tacos from back home. This is by no means a traditional Mexican taco, but it is my Mexican-inspired twist on the classic American taco.

1 cup plus 2 tablespoons
   vegetable oil, divided
½ medium onion,
   finely chopped
1 serrano chile, seeded and
   finely chopped
2 garlic cloves, minced
1½ pounds ground beef
1 tablespoon ancho
   chile powder

1 teaspoon ground cumin
¾ teaspoon salt
½ teaspoon freshly ground
   black pepper
½ teaspoon
   crushed oregano
3 roma tomatoes, chopped
2 cups *Refried Beans*
   (page 96)
12 to 18 corn tortillas

Shredded lettuce,
   for garnish
Chopped tomato,
   for garnish
Shredded asadero or
   Chihuahua cheese,
   for garnish
Salsa Taquera Roja
   (page 143), for serving

1 In a large skillet, heat 2 tablespoons of the oil over medium-high heat. Add the onion and serrano chile and sauté, stirring occasionally, for 2 to 3 minutes, until the onion turns translucent. Add the garlic and sauté an additional 30 seconds. Add the ground beef and cook for about 5 minutes, until no longer pink. Add the chile powder, cumin, salt, pepper, and oregano, stirring until well combined. Stir in the tomatoes. Cover, reduce the heat to low, and simmer for 18 to 20 minutes, until all of the liquid has evaporated. Uncover and increase the heat to medium-high. Continue to cook the beef until lightly browned. Remove from the heat.

2 While the meat is cooking, reheat the refried beans.

3 On a comal, griddle, or nonstick skillet, heat the tortillas over medium-high heat for 30 to 45 seconds, until soft and pliable. Transfer to a platter. Spoon about 3 tablespoons of ground beef filling down the center of each tortilla. Fold in half to form a taco and secure with a toothpick, if desired.

4 In a large skillet, heat the remaining 1 cup of the oil over medium-high heat. Fry the tacos, three or four at a time, until golden and crisp on both sides. Transfer the tacos to a paper towel–lined plate to drain any excess oil. Remove the toothpicks before serving.

5 Place three tacos on each plate. Top with 2 tablespoons of *Refried Beans*. Garnish with shredded lettuce, chopped tomato, and a sprinkling of shredded cheese. Serve with the salsa.

TIP Save time in the cocina by serving the meat in taco shells instead of using the corn tortillas and frying the tacos.

TAQUITOS DE QUESO TRICOLOR

YIELD: 4 TO 6 SERVINGS   PREP TIME: 10 MINUTES   COOK TIME: 15 MINUTES

Taquitos de Queso *are another of my childhood favorites. Pappy made them because he loved the flavor of the fried cheese, while Gramm usually made them when we were running low on groceries. To serve* Taquitos de Queso Tricolor *means to top them with a trio of salsas in the same colors of the Mexican flag: red, white, and green—* Salsa Taquera Roja *(page 143), Mexican crema, and* Salsa Verde *(pages 145 and 146).*

1 cup *Salsa Taquera Roja* (page 143)
1 cup *Mild* or *Spicy Salsa Verde* (pages 145 and 146)
12 corn tortillas
3 cups crumbled queso fresco, divided
½ cup vegetable oil, for frying
1 cup Mexican crema or sour cream
Frijoles Adobados (page 98)
Arroz Mexicano (page 100)

1 In seperate medium saucepans, heat each salsa over medium-high heat. Set aside.

2 On a comal, griddle, or nonstick skillet, heat the tortillas over medium-high heat for 30 to 45 seconds, until soft and pliable. Transfer to a platter. Spoon about 3 tablespoons of crumbled queso fresco close to the edge of each tortilla. Tightly roll the tortillas to form taquitos. Secure with toothpick, if desired.

3 In a medium nonstick skillet, heat the oil over medium-high heat. Fry the taquitos, 3 to 4 at a time, until golden and crisp on all sides. Transfer the taquitos to a paper towel–lined plate to drain any excess oil. Remove toothpicks before serving.

4 Place three or four taquitos on each plate. Spoon the crema down the center (crosswise) of the taquitos. Spoon *Salsa Taquera Roja* to the right of the *crema*, and *Salsa Verde* to the left. Garnish with the remaining queso fresco. Serve with *Frijoles Adobados* and *Arroz Mexicano*.

TIP *Omit the Mexican crema and top taquitos with just red and green salsa for* Taquitos Divorciados.

SOFT, FRIED, OR HARD TACO SHELLS?

▽▽ ◇ ▽▽ ◇ ▽▽ ◇ ▽▽ ◇ ▽▽ ◇ ▽▽▽▽▽▽▽ ◇ ▽▽▽▽ ◇ ▽▽

If you've ever wondered why traditional Mexican tacos are usually served with two stacked soft corn tortillas, it's to ensure that there's a resistant base that won't fall apart under the weight of the filling, garnishes, and salsas. In fact, once upon a time, my husband's hometown served tacos with three stacked corn tortillas and three to a plate (they called them tercias, or thirds). In some instances, like for tacos de pescado in Baja California and tacos de cabrito asado in Nuevo León, tacos are served on a single soft flour tortilla.

Tacos dorados and flautas are deep-fried in vegetable oil or manteca, although you can get the same crisp results at home by baking the tacos in the oven. These tacos are made with regular-sized corn tortillas.

The hard U-shaped taco shells popularized by certain fast-food restaurant chains are nonexistent in Mexico, with the exception of

some border towns. And even though I am surrounded by almost every taco imaginable where I live in Mexico, I am still a Southern California girl at heart who will always have a soft spot for hard-shell tacos.

No matter what kind of taco shell you prefer, most of the recipes included in this book are easily adaptable to fit your personal preference. What really matters is that you spend a nice meal with great company and good food.

NINE
DRINKS

▽ ▽

There is a world of thirst-quenching aguas frescas (light nonalcoholic beverages), warm comforting beverages, and fun Mexican cocktails made with tequila, mezcal, and cerveza to be discovered.

Aguas frescas that are made from fresh fruits, dried flowers, or grains—like rice, barley, and oats—are refreshing alternatives to sodas. While there are an endless number of flavor possibilities, the three most popular agua fresca flavors are horchata *(rice and cinnamon; page 187),* jamaica *(hibiscus; page 188), and* tamarindo *(tamarind; page 189). These three flavors are often found side-by-side at taquerías and Mexican restaurants. Lightly sweetened and oh-so-refreshing, aguas frescas are the perfect accompaniment to any Mexican feast. And best of all, they're alcohol-free, so the whole family can enjoy.*

But if you're looking for an adults-only beverage, we've got plenty of those as well: from classic margaritas and palomas to mojitos made with mezcal to Mexican beer micheladas.

On cold winter nights, you're sure to enjoy Mexican Hot Chocolate *(champurrado; page 200).*

DRINKS

CLASSIC LIME MARGARITA

YIELD: 1 SERVING   PREP TIME: 5 MINUTES

Without a doubt, margaritas are the most popular tequila cocktail. Not only are they incredibly delicious, with the subtle sweetness of the agave tequila melding with the citruses, but margaritas are also one of the most versatile cocktails out there: They can be served shaken, frozen, or stirred, and their flavor profile can range from fruity and sweet to salty and spicy.

I enjoy margaritas in all forms and flavors, but my favorite margarita will always be the classic—made with lime juice, tequila, and an orange-flavored liqueur (be it Grand Marnier, Cointreau, or Licor 43)—served on the rocks.

Making a classic lime margarita is so easy, with just a handful of ingredients, that there really is no need to use that horrible neon-colored concoction called "margarita mix," which is full of artificial flavoring. Always use fresh lime juice (nothing out of a bottle).

A good-quality tequila is a must, whether you're using tequila blanco, silver, añejo, or reposado. Some of my all-time favorite tequila brands include Don Julio, San Matías, and Herradura. But no matter what kind of tequila you use, be sure the bottle says "100% agave."

Two final suggestions: Chill your glasses in the freezer about 30 minutes before happy hour, and feel free to adjust how much of each of the ingredients you add to fit your personal taste. ¡Salud! (Cheers!)

➔

1 tablespoon coarse salt

2 lime wedges

2 ounces fresh lime juice

2 ounces tequila

1 ounce orange liqueur
(Grand Marnier,
Cointreau, or Licor 43)

1 ounce simple syrup
(optional)

Spread the salt in a thin layer on a saucer. Moisten the rim of 1 chilled lowball glass with a lime wedge and press the moistened rim into the coarse salt. Fill the glass with ice. Add the lime juice, tequila, orange liqueur, and simple syrup (if using). Stir gently to combine. Top with a pinch any remaining salt and garnish with a lime wedge.

TIP *Prepare your own simple syrup by simmering equal parts (1 cup each) of granulated sugar and water in a small saucepan over medium heat until the sugar has dissolved completely. Cool completely before using.*

TAQUERÍA TACOS

HORCHATA DE AVENA

YIELD: 8 CUPS   PREP TIME: 5 MINUTES

Made with rice and cinnamon, horchata is one of the most popular flavors of Mexican aguas frescas. Because the rice settles into a grainy residue, I prefer to use oats to make my horchata, as it grinds into a finer powder (when oats are used, the horchata is sometimes also called agua de avena*). The addition of sweetened condensed milk not only sweetens this traditional beverage, but also intensifies the creamy flavor and consistency.*

1 cup old-fashioned oats
6 cups water
1 cinnamon stick
1 (14-ounce) can sweetened
    condensed milk
Granulated sugar (optional)

Blend the oats, water, and cinnamon stick in a blender until smooth. Strain the purée into a 2-quart pitcher. Add the sweetened condensed milk and stir until it dissolves completely. Sweeten with granulated sugar, if desired. Refrigerate until ready to serve. Serve in tall glasses filled with ice.

 Turn this into a grown-up treat by adding a shot of rum to each glass before serving.

DAIRY FREE

VEG

AGUA DE JAMAICA

♡ ♡

YIELD: 8 CUPS   PREP TIME: 30 MINUTES TO 24 HOURS

Dried hibiscus flowers make a delicious and refreshing drink, often found in large glass vitroleros (pitchers) alongside Horchata de Avena *(page 187) and* Agua de Tamarindo *(page 189) in taquerías and Mexican restaurants. Agua de jamaica can be made two ways: steeping the dried flowers in boiling water, which makes a more concentrated flavor with a deep jewel-toned color, and steeping in room-temperature water, which makes an agua fresca with a lighter flavor and color.*

1 cup dried flor de jamaica
8 cups water, divided
½ to ¾ cup
    granulated sugar

TO MAKE ON THE STOVE TOP

1 In a medium saucepan, add the dried hibiscus flowers and 3 cups of the water and bring to a boil over medium-high heat. Remove from the heat and let cool to room temperature.

2 Strain the agua de jamaica concentrate into a 2-quart pitcher. Stir in the remaining 5 cups of the water and sweeten with granulated sugar. Refrigerate until ready to serve. Serve in tall glasses filled with ice.

NO-COOK METHOD

Fill a 2-quart pitcher with water. Stir in the dried hibiscus flowers; refrigerate for at least 3 hours and up to overnight. Using a slotted spoon, remove the flowers. Sweeten with granulated sugar. Serve in tall glasses filled with ice.

TIP *Don't discard the rehydrated flowers! They can be used to make quesadillas or Hibiscus Flower Tacos.*

TAQUERÍA TACOS

AGUA DE TAMARINDO

YIELD: 8 CUPS   PREP TIME: 60 MINUTES   COOK TIME: 20 MINUTES

Tamarind pods are a sweet and tart fruit popular in Indian and Thai cuisines. In Mexico, tamarind is used to make sauces, paletas, ponche navideño *(a hot Christmas cider), and a deliciously refreshing agua fresca. The hardest part to making Agua de Tamarindo at home is taking the time to peel the pods. Simply remove the hard outer shell, the stems, and the veins. If you encounter a few stubborn pieces of shell or vein, don't worry, they can be easily removed once the tamarind has been cooked.*

8 ounces tamarind pods, shelled, stemmed, and deveined

8 cups water

½ to ¾ cup granulated sugar

1 In a medium saucepan, bring the tamarind pods and water to a simmer over medium heat. Simmer for 20 minutes. Remove from the heat. Using a potato masher or the back of a wooden spoon, gently press the tamarind to break up the pulp, removing the seeds and any traces of shell or veins. Cool to room temperature.

2 Blend the cooled tamarind and its water in a blender until smooth. Pour into a 2-quart pitcher. Add enough water to fill the pitcher, if necessary. Sweeten with granulated sugar. Refrigerate until ready to serve. Serve in tall glasses with ice.

TIP Make paletas by freezing leftover Agua de Tamarindo in ice-pop molds for a cool summertime treat.

DAIRY FREE

VEG

DRINKS

DAIRY FREE

QUICK & EASY

MICHELADA

v v v v v v v v v v v v v v v v v v v v v v v v v v v v v v v v v v v v v v v v v v v v v v v v v v v

YIELD: 1 SERVING   PREP TIME: 5 MINUTES

A michelada is a mouthwatering beer cocktail flavored with Maggi Jugo Seasoning Sauce, Worcestershire sauce, lime juice, and Clamato (a clam and tomato juice) and is often referred to as the Mexican Bloody Mary. Like many Mexican recipes, micheladas and the ingredients used can vary from region to region. In recent years, playful garnishes from skewers of grilled shrimp to cacahuate japones *(roasted peanuts with a crunchy coating) and tart gummy candies have become very popular. I prefer to make my micheladas with a dark Mexican beer, but a light-hued lager also works well in this cocktail.*

Tajín
1 lime wedge
Juice of 1 lime
½ teaspoon Maggi Jugo
  Seasoning Sauce
¼ teaspoon
  Worcestershire sauce
¼ teaspoon bottled hot
  sauce (Tabasco or
  Valentina)
¼ cup Clamato, chilled
¼ teaspoon salt
⅛ teaspoon freshly ground
  black pepper (optional)
1 (12-ounce) bottle
  light or dark Mexican
  beer, chilled

Spread a thin layer of Tajín on a saucer. Moisten the rim of a frosted beer mug with the lime wedge and press the moistened rim into the Tajín. Add the lime juice, jugo Maggi, Worcestershire sauce, hot sauce, Clamato, salt, and black pepper (if using) to the glass. Slowly pour in the Mexican beer.

TIP *Maggi Jugo and Clamato are readily available in supermarkets. Have fun playing around with this recipe by substituting tamarind concentrate or mango nectar for the Clamato. Or you can adjust the seasoning by adding a few drops of chipotle salsa or salsa de chamoy (a sweet and tangy salsa) to the mix.*

VAMPIRO

Vampiro is my all-time favorite tequila cocktail. Grapefruit soda and lime juice are combined with the real star of this cocktail—sangrita, a salty-sweet tequila chaser. I love sangrita so much that I even love alcohol-free versions of this drink. I tend to shy away from recommending certain brands, but when it comes to sangrita I highly recommend Viuda de Sanchez (available online), which gets its bright color and distinct flavor from ground chile de árbol.

Tajín
1 lime wedge
Juice of 1 lime
¼ teaspoon salt
1 to 2 ounces tequila
2 ounces sangrita
Grapefruit-flavored
   soda, chilled

Spread a thin layer of Tajín on a saucer. Moisten a chilled highball glass with the lime wedge and press the moistened rim in the Tajín. Fill the glass with ice. Add the lime juice, tequila, and sangrita to the glass. Top with the grapefruit-flavored soda.

TIP If grapefruit-flavored soda is too sweet for your taste, add a splash of chilled sparkling water before adding the soda.

CUCUMBER LIME MARGARITA

YIELD: 4 SERVINGS   PREP TIME: 10 MINUTES

Slices of cucumbers seasoned with salt, chile powder, and lime juice have long been a popular snack in Mexico. Margarita de Pepino y Limón, as this drink is known in Spanish, is a grown-up version of that tasty snack. The combination of cucumber, lime, and chile powder makes for a refreshing cocktail that is sure to impress guests at your next summer barbecue.

Tajín
1 lime wedge
1 large cucumber, peeled, seeded, and cut into large chunks
½ cup freshly squeezed lime juice
½ cup simple syrup
1 cup tequila reposado
½ cup orange liqueur
Coarse salt (optional)

1 Spread a thin layer of Tajín on a saucer. Moisten the rims of four chilled lowball glasses with the lime wedge, and press the moistened rims into the Tajín. Fill the glasses with ice and chill in the freezer until ready to serve.

2 Blend the cucumber, lime juice, and simple syrup in a blender until smooth. In a pitcher, add the cucumber purée, tequila, and orange liqueur, stirring gently to combine. Pour the margarita mix into the ice-filled, chilled lowball glasses. Top each glass with a pinch coarse salt (if using).

Purée the cucumber, lime juice, simple syrup, and tequila in a blender with 4 cups of ice for frozen cucumber margaritas.

AGUA DE GUAYABA

YIELD: 8 SERVINGS   PREP TIME: 5 MINUTES

You're going to love this fragrant agua fresca made with fresh guavas and cinnamon. The cinnamon not only complements the flavor of the guavas, it helps intensify their natural flavor. Any kind of guayaba (guava) will do for this recipe. Pale yellow guavas will result in a light-hued agua fresca, while guavas with a pink center will result in a vibrantly colored beverage.

8 fresh guavas, cut into quarters
1 cinnamon stick
6 to 8 cups water, divided
½ to ¾ cup granulated sugar

Blend the guavas, cinnamon stick, and 4 cups of the water in a blender until smooth. Strain the mixture into a 2-quart pitcher. Add enough water to fill the pitcher, if necessary. Sweeten with the sugar, stirring until the sugar dissolves completely. Refrigerate until ready to serve. Serve in tall glasses filled with ice.

TIP While the cinnamon gives the agua fresca a spicy heat that I crave, the drink is still delicious without it, if you're not a fan.

NARANJADA MINERAL

YIELD: 1 SERVING   PREP TIME: 5 MINUTES

Naranjada Mineral *is an alcohol-free drink that has recently been popularized. Made with sparkling water—*agua mineral en español—*this is the perfect drink for when you want something slightly sweet and fizzy, but not necessarily a soda. This recipe can easily be doubled or tripled to serve a crowd.*

1 tablespoon
   granulated sugar
2 ounces fresh orange juice
8 ounces sparkling water or
   club soda, chilled
Coarse salt (optional)

In a tall glass, combine the sugar and orange juice, stirring until the sugar dissolves completely. Add ice and pour in enough sparkling water to fill the glass. Top off with a pinch of the salt, if desired.

TIP *For a Limonada Mineral, substitute freshly squeezed lime juice for the orange juice.*

PIÑA COLADA AGUA FRESCA

YIELD: 8 SERVINGS   PREP TIME: 10 MINUTES

This Piña Colada Agua Fresca is a family-friendly version of the classic cocktail. Made with fresh pineapple and shredded coconut, this beverage is so creamy and delicious you won't even notice that there isn't any alcohol. (Although you can always add a shot of rum to your glass before serving.) The cream of coconut adds more coconut flavor and sweetness, as well as a creamy consistency for a dreamy, tropical delight.

2 cups fresh
   pineapple chunks
1 cup shredded coconut
6 to 8 cups water, divided
1 cup coconut cream
Granulated sugar (optional)
Maraschino cherries
   (optional)

Blend the pineapple, coconut, and 4 cups of the water in a blender until smooth. Strain the purée into a 2-quart pitcher. Stir in the coconut cream and enough water to fill the pitcher. Sweeten with the sugar, if desired. Refrigerate until ready to serve. Serve in glasses filled with ice. Garnish with a Maraschino cherry, if desired.

TIP *Enjoy this tropical agua fresca even in the winter by substituting 1 (15.5-ounce) can of pineapple chunks for the fresh.*

PALOMA

YIELD: 1 SERVING   PREP TIME: 5 MINUTES

This traditional tequila cocktail made with grapefruit soda is how tequila is most often served in Mexico. For years I made this cocktail using only tequila, lime juice, salt, and grapefruit-flavored soda. But recently, while attending El Grito *(Mexico's Independence Day celebration), the barman topped off my cocktail with a splash of sparkling water. That toned down the sweetness of the soda and made my cocktail unexpectedly more refreshing. I've been making my palomas that way ever since.*

¼ teaspoon salt, plus more for the rim
1 lime wedge
Juice of 1 lime
2 ounces tequila
Grapefruit-flavored soda, chilled
Sparkling water, chilled

Spread a thin layer of the salt on a saucer. Moisten the rim of a chilled glass with the lime wedge and press the moistened rim into salt. Fill the glass with ice. Add the lime juice and tequila; stir gently to combine. Top with grapefruit-flavored soda and a splash of sparkling water.

TIP   *In some parts of Mexico substituting vodka for the tequila transforms this cocktail into a* rusa, *while in other parts a* rusa *refers to an alcohol-free version of the* paloma.

CANTARITO

The Cantarito is a fun take on the classic Paloma (page 196). Made with fresh lime, orange, and grapefruit juice, this cocktail is often served in cantaritos de barro (small clay jugs). The Cantarito is especially popular when the fair is in town or during the Independence Day celebrations across Mexico. The best part of buying a cantarito at the fair is that after you've finished your cocktail, you have a cute clay jug to take home and add to your growing collection.

Tajín
1 lime wedge
Juice of 1 lime
1 ounce fresh orange juice
1 ounce fresh
    grapefruit juice
¼ teaspoon salt
2 ounces tequila
Grapefruit-flavored
    soda, chilled
Lime, orange, and grapefruit
    wedges, for garnish

Spread a thin layer of Tajín on a saucer. Moisten the rim of a cantarito or tall glass with the lime wedge and press the moistened rim into the Tajín. Add the lime juice, orange juice, grapefruit juice, and salt, and stir gently to combine. Fill the cantarito or glass with ice. Add the tequila and top off with grapefruit-flavored soda. Garnish with lime, orange, and grapefruit wedges.

TIP: If you are serving this cocktail in clay cantaritos, soak the cantaritos in cold water at least one hour before serving.

DAIRY FREE

VEG

QUICK & EASY

DRINKS

CLERICOT

YIELD: 12 SERVINGS   PREP TIME: 5 MINUTES

In Mexico, we also enjoy a few cocktails made with something other than cerveza or tequila. Clericot is similar to sangría in that it is a wine-based cocktail made with chopped fruit, except it is not as sweet and has a much lighter taste than sangría. In our family we like to make our clericot with only diced apples and oranges, but you can also add fruits like strawberries and nectarines. This cocktail is perfect for an afternoon picnic or for Sunday brunch with family.

2 Granny Smith
  apples, diced
1 orange, diced
1 (750 ml) bottle red
  wine, chilled
¼ to ½ cup
  granulated sugar
¼ cup freshly squeezed
  lime juice
2 cups sparkling
  water, chilled

In a 2-quart pitcher, stir together the apples, orange, red wine, sugar (to your taste; I prefer to use the lesser amount), and lime juice. Refrigerate until ready to serve. Add sparkling water just before serving. Serve chilled clericot in glasses, making sure to get plenty of the fruit.

 Too light for your taste? Stir in 1 cup of vodka with the red wine.

MANGO MEZCAL MOJITO

YIELD: 1 SERVING   PREP TIME: 5 MINUTES

I remember all the times my grandparents bought bottles of "that stuff with the worm in it" during our many trips to Mexico to visit family. My grandparents never opened a bottle for themselves, but they loved sharing bottles of real Mexican mezcal with friends and neighbors for birthdays and holidays. It wasn't until I moved to Mexico that I had my first sip of mezcal. I don't know what I was expecting, but the sweet, smoky flavor was far better than I had hoped for and imagined. Over the years, I've had fun dreaming up new cocktails, my favorite being this mezcal mojito made with fresh mango.

Juice of 1 lime
1 tablespoon sugar
6 fresh mint leaves
¼ cup chopped fresh mango
2 ounces mezcal
Sparkling water, chilled

In a tall glass, combine the lime juice, sugar, mint leaves, and mango. Lightly mash the mango and mint leaves into the sugar and lime juice using a cocktail muddler or fork. Fill the glass with ice. Pour in the mezcal and top off with sparkling water.

TIP Summer is my favorite time of the year to enjoy a refreshing mojito because of the wide variety of fruits that are in season. Switch up the flavor of your mojito by substituting fresh strawberries, raspberries, or nectarines for the mango.

DRINKS

MEXICAN HOT CHOCOLATE

YIELD: 6 SERVINGS   PREP TIME: 5 MINUTES   COOK TIME: 20 MINUTES

Champurrado is a traditional Mexican atole flavored with chocolate and thickened with masa harina. Think of it as a thicker cinnamon-spiced hot cocoa with a slightly grainy texture. Mexican chocolate is readily available in supermarkets and often found in the same aisle as other hot chocolate drinks. Just look for a yellow and red hexagon-shaped box.

½ cup masa harina
3 cups milk
3 cups water
1 (3-ounce) tablet
  Mexican chocolate, cut
  into wedges
1 (3-inch) cinnamon stick
¼ to ½ cup sugar

1 Blend the masa harina and 1 cup of the milk in a blender until smooth. Set aside.

2 In a medium saucepan, heat the remaining 2 cups of the milk, the water, chocolate, and cinnamon stick over medium heat, stirring occasionally, for 8 to 10 minutes, until the chocolate has completely melted. Remove the cinnamon stick.

3 Stir in the masa harina mixture and sweeten with the sugar. Stirring constantly with a wire whisk to prevent lumps from forming, continue simmering for 12 to 15 minutes, until the champurrado starts to thicken. Remove from the heat.

For a smoother textured hot chocolate, substitute ⅓ cup cornstarch for the masa harina. Also, to substitute the 3-ounce tablet of Mexican chocolate, use ¼ cup cocoa powder, 1½ teaspoons ground cinnamon, and ¼ teaspoon almond extract.

TEQUILA VS MEZCAL

Tequila and mezcal are Mexico's gifts to cocktail lovers everywhere. While both spirits are derived from the agave plant, each has a set of unique qualities that set them apart.

First produced sometime during the 16th century near the town of Tequila, Jalisco, tequila is made solely from Weber's agave azúl (blue agave) and is the more popular of the two spirits. While most brands of tequilas are still produced in the state of Jalisco, certified Mexican tequila can be produced in five Mexican states: Jalisco, Michoacán, Guanajuato, Nayarit, and Tamaulipas. Tequila is often distilled twice before being aged in wood barrels for as few as two months to as long as two years (sometimes even longer).

With so many tequila brands on the market now, it can be hard to decide what kind of tequila to buy. If a tequila bottle says it was produced in Baja California or Arizona, it's not the real thing; stick to tequilas produced in the five states mentioned earlier. Always look for labels that say "100% agave." Anything less is just that: a lesser quality tequila. Stay away from tequilas labelled "oro" or "young," as they are also of lesser quality than tequilas blanco, silver, añejo, and reposado.

Unlike tequila, mezcal can be made from more than a dozen varieties of agave. Its production is still very much an artisanal process, though also always 100% agave. Mezcal can only be produced in the states of Durango, Guanajuato, Guerrero, San Luis Potosí, Zacatecas, Tamaulipas, Michoacán, and Oaxaca—the latter being where the majority of mezcal is produced. Mezcal is the spirit known for having a worm in the bottle, but it is a practice used by lower quality brands as the worm actually breaks down the flavor and quality of the mezcal.

Both tequila and mezcal are delicious served as shots or mixed in a variety of cocktails, but the sweet flavor of the agave is best enjoyed served alone on the rocks and savored slowly like a fine wine.

APPENDIX A
MEASUREMENT CONVERSIONS

▽▽ ▽ ▽ ▽ ▽ ▽ ▽▽ ▽ ▽ ▽ ▽ ▽ ▽ ▽ ▽▽▽ ▽ ▽ ▽ ▽▽▽ ▽ ▽ ▽▽ ▽ ▽ ▽

VOLUME EQUIVALENTS (LIQUID)

US STANDARD	US STANDARD (OUNCES)	METRIC (APPROXIMATE)
2 tablespoons	1 fl. oz.	30 mL
¼ cup	2 fl. oz.	60 mL
½ cup	4 fl. oz.	120 mL
1 cup	8 fl. oz.	240 mL
1½ cups	12 fl. oz.	355 mL
2 cups or 1 pint	16 fl. oz.	475 mL
4 cups or 1 quart	32 fl. oz.	1 L
1 gallon	128 fl. oz.	4 L

OVEN TEMPERATURES

FAHRENHEIT	CELSIUS (APPROXIMATE)
250°F	120°C
300°F	150°C
325°F	165°C
350°F	180°C
375°F	190°C
400°F	200°C
425°F	220°C
450°F	230°C

VOLUME EQUIVALENTS (DRY)

US STANDARD	METRIC (APPROXIMATE)
⅛ teaspoon	0.5 mL
¼ teaspoon	1 mL
½ teaspoon	2 mL
¾ teaspoon	4 mL
1 teaspoon	5 mL
1 tablespoon	15 mL
¼ cup	59 mL
⅓ cup	79 mL
½ **cup**	118 mL
⅔ cup	156 mL
¾ cup	177 mL
1 cup	235 mL
2 cups or 1 pint	475 mL
3 cups	700 mL
4 cups or 1 quart	1 L

WEIGHT EQUIVALENTS

US STANDARD	METRIC (APPROXIMATE)
½ ounce	15 g
1 ounce	30 g
2 ounces	60 g
4 ounces	115 g
8 ounces	225 g
12 ounces	340 g
16 ounces or 1 pound	455 g

INGREDIENT DICTIONARY

▽ ▽

avena *oats*

arrachera *skirt steak*

arroz *rice*

asadero *melting cheese*

asado *roast*

atún *tuna*

barbacoa *barbecue*

birria *slow-roasted*

bistec *steak*

brochetas *skewers*

cabrito *young goat*

cacahuate *peanut*

calabacitas *mixed zucchini, tomatoes, and corn*

caldo *broth*

camarones *shrimp*

camote *sweet potato*

carne *meat, usually beef*

carnicerías *butcher shops*

carnitas *goat meat*

cazuela *casserole*

cebollas *onions*

cerveza *beer*

champiñones *mushrooms*

chicharrón *pork rinds*

chilorio *shredded pork*

cóctel *cocktail*

costillita *spareribs*

discadas *meat cooked over a large disc, or wok*

dorados *rolled tacos*

dulce *sweet*

ejotes *green beans*

ensalada *salad*

espinacas *spinach*

flor *flower*

frijoles *beans*

guisados *stews*

guayaba *guava*

hojas *leaves*

huevos *eggs*

Jamaica *hibiscus*

langosta *lobster*

límon *lemon*

machaca *dried beef*

maíz *corn*

manteca *lard*

masa harina *wheat flour*

mojo *sauce*

paletas *ice pops*

papas *potatoes*

pescadería *fish market*

pescado *fish*

pipián *pumpkin seed sauce*

piña *pineapple*

plancha *griddle*

pollo *chicken*

pulpo *octopus*

queso *cheese*

rajas *sliced peppers*

requesón *a style of fresh cheese*

salpicón *medley*

sopa *soup*

tamarindo *tamarind*

torta *Mexican-style sandwich*

ACKNOWLEDGEMENTS

▽ ▽ ▽ ▽ ▽ ▽ ▽ ▽ ▽ ▽ ▽ ▽ ▽ ▽ ▽ ▽ ▽ ▽ ▽ ▽

I could not have written this book without the love, support, and encouragement of my wonderful husband Alfonso and our four children Hope, Nicholas, Ashley, and Jack. *Gracias por siempre creer en mí y por apoyarme en cada momento. Los quiero con todo mi corazón y les dedico este libro.* (Thank you for always believing in me and for supporting me in every moment. I love you with all my heart and dedicate this book to you.) I am forever grateful to my grandparents, Anita and Jesus, for sharing their love of la cocina with me, and for showing me that the key ingredient to any meal, no matter how simple or elaborate, is the love with which it is prepared. I also thank my *suegra* (mother-in-law),

Doña Esperanza, for teaching me how to make the traditional Mexican dishes my husband grew up with, which have become some of my most cherished recipes. There isn't a day that goes by that I don't think about my grandparents and *suegra*, and the anecdotes behind every recipe. To my in-laws, I thank them for letting me pick their brains and for sharing their knowledge of Mexican history. I thank my friends and family for their continued support and for answering my endless questions on Facebook. And finally, a big thank you to the awesome team of people at Callisto Media for making my dream of writing a cookbook come true.

INDEX

▽ ▽ ▽ ▽ ▽ ▽

CPSIA information can be obtained
at www.ICGtesting.com
Printed in the USA
BVOW05s1424221116
468621BV00002B/2/P